THE LIFE OF
ST. FRANCIS OF ASSISI

St. Francis of Assisi
c.1181—1226
Founder of the Franciscan Order

THE LIFE OF
ST. FRANCIS OF ASSISI

by

ST. BONAVENTURE

(FROM THE "LEGENDA SANCTI FRANCISCI")

EDITED, WITH A PREFACE, BY HIS EMINENCE
CARDINAL MANNING

"To him that thirsteth, I will give of the fountain of the water of life, freely. He that shall overcome shall possess these things, and I will be his God; and he shall be my son."

—Apocalypse 21:6-7

TAN BOOKS AND PUBLISHERS, INC.
Rockford, Illinois 61105

Imprimatur: ✠ Henry Edward Manning
Archbishop of Westminster
December 8, 1867

This text was originally published in English circa 1867. The TAN edition was published in 1988 by photographic reproduction from the 1925 edition of Burns Oates & Washbourne Ltd., London by agreement with Burns & Oates Ltd., Tunbridge Wells, England. The TAN edition was retypeset in 2008.

Library of Congress Catalog Card No.: 88-50746

ISBN 978-0-89555-343-0

Cover Illustration: Picture of St. Francis, formerly attributed to Simone Martini, but now more probably to Donato of Siena. (Fresco in the Lower Church of San Francesco at Assisi.) Photographed by Leonard von Matt. At first glance the eyes of this picture may appear to be severe, but a close examination will reveal that they reflect profound spirituality.

Printed and bound in the United States of America.

TAN BOOKS AND PUBLISHERS, INC.
P.O. Box 424
Rockford, Illinois 61105
1988

"But as many as received him, he gave them power to be made the sons of God, to them that believe in his name. Who are born, not of blood, nor of the will of the flesh, nor of the will of man, but of God."
—John 1:12-13

Preface to the First Edition

THE life of a Saint, written by a Saint, as the life of St. Paul of the Cross written by his companion, the Blessed Strambi, speaks to the heart with a vital power which no work of merely natural genius can command. It has a twofold operation of the Spirit of God with it, both in the subject and in the writer. Such is, in an eminent degree, the Life of St. Francis, by St. Bonaventure—the life of the Seraphic Patriarch written by the Seraphic Doctor. Among uninspired books there are few that breathe more sensibly the love of God. There is a light and a sweetness about it which is not of this world. The anecdote of St. Thomas visiting St. Bonaventure's cell, and finding him in ecstasy, is too well known to need recital. St. Bonaventure was then writing the Life of St. Francis, and it was on these very pages that he was intent when St. Thomas drew back from the door, saying, "Let us leave a Saint to work for a Saint." It is in this same spirit of love and reverence that we ought to read this book.

✠ HENRY EDWARD,
Archbishop of Westminster.

Feast of the Immaculate Conception,
1867.

Prologue

HE grace of God our Saviour hath appeared in these our latter days in His faithful and devout servant Francis, and hath been manifested through him to all those who are truly humble and lovers of holy poverty; who, honoring and devoutly adoring the superabundance of the divine mercy, which was so bountifully poured forth upon him, have been taught by his example to forsake all impiety and worldly desires, to conform their lives to the life of Christ, and with intense and burning desire to thirst after the hope of heavenly beatitude. For so graciously did God look upon this truly poor and contrite man, that He not only raised the poor and needy from the vile dust of worldly conversation, but also set him to be a light to the faithful, making him to become a true professor, leader, and herald of evangelical perfection, that, bearing witness to the light, he might prepare before the Lord a way of light and peace in the hearts of the faithful. For, shining like a morning star in the midst of a dark cloud, he enlightened by the bright rays of his pure doctrine and holy life those who lay in darkness and in the shadow of death, and thus guided them onwards by his bright shining to the perfect day. And like the glorious rainbow set in the darkness of the clouds, he came forth as the angel of true peace and the sign of the covenant between God and man, bringing glad tidings of peace and salvation: being sent by God, like the Precursor of Christ, to prepare in the desert of this world the highway of holy poverty, and by word and example to preach penance to men.

Thus prevented by the gifts of heavenly grace, enriched with the merits of invincible virtue, filled with the spirit of prophecy, and ordained to the angelic office of declaring good tidings, burning with seraphic fire, and raised above all human things in the fiery chariot of divine love, it may be reasonably affirmed from the clear testimony of His whole life that he came in the spirit and power of Elias.

We may also say that he was truly shadowed forth by that other friend of Christ, the Apostle and Evangelist St. John, under the similitude of the angel whom he saw ascending from the east with the sign of the living God. Under this figure we may assuredly discern Francis, the servant, herald, and messenger of God, the beloved of Christ, the pattern for our imitation, the wonder of the world, if we carefully observe and mark the excellency of his marvellous sanctity, by which, during his life, he imitated the purity of the Angels, so that he may be set forth as an example to all the perfect followers of Christ.

And we are not only moved firmly to believe this, and confidently to affirm it by that office which he exercised in his own person, inviting all men to tears and penance, clothing himself in sackcloth, girding himself with a cord, shaving his head, and signing, with the salutary Sign of the Cross, the foreheads of those who mourned over their offenses against God, even as the Angel was wont to mark the foreheads of men with the mysterious character of Tau: we recognize him, indeed, by the habit which he wore, bearing the outward semblance of the Cross, but far more certainly by the seal of the likeness of the living God, even of Jesus Christ crucified, which was impressed upon his body, neither by natural power, nor artificial contrivance, but by the marvellous efficacy of the Spirit of the living God.

I know myself, then, to be most unworthy and unequal to describe the life of this most venerable man,
thus set forth for the imitation of the faithful; nor
should I ever have attempted such a task, but for my
ardent love for my brethren; being moved thereto by
the urgent request of our General Chapter, and no less
by the devotion which I am bound to bear to this our
holy Father, by whose merits and invocation I was (as
I well remember), while yet a child, delivered from the
jaws of death. Were I then to be silent in his praise,
I should fear justly to incur the charge of ingratitude.
Good reason, indeed, have I to undertake this labor,
that so, in return for the bodily and spiritual life preserved to me by God for the sake of his merits and
virtues, I, on my part, may preserve as best I may
(albeit imperfectly), the acts, words, and virtues of his
life, which are scattered and dispersed in divers places,
and so gather them together, that they may not perish with the lives of those who lived and conversed
with him on earth.

Having, therefore, to set forth the life of so holy a
man, that I might obtain certain knowledge of all things
relating to it, I went to the place where he was born,
and learned, from many who had been familiar with
him whilst he was yet on earth, the manner of his life
and conversation, and of his departure out of this world.
I examined all these things with great diligence, and
conferred thereupon with some who, having been his
chief disciples, had full knowledge of his marvellous
sanctity, and who are worthy of all credit for their
approved virtue and perfect knowledge of the truth.
Now, in describing all these things, and the sublime
and wonderful deeds which God was pleased to work
by this His servant, I have judged it fitting to avoid
all curious ornaments of style and vain eloquence of
words—believing that the devotion of the reader will

be enkindled rather by a pure and simple idiom than by an ornamental phraseology. Neither have I been careful, in weaving the web of my story, to follow the order of time; but, to avoid the confusion of subjects which might thence arise, I have rather studied to follow such an order as would string together facts of the same class and kind, although they may have taken place at different times. The beginning, therefore, and course of this life, and finally the end of it, shall be related in fifteen chapters, the contents of which, for greater clearness and distinctness, are set down below.

Contents

Chapter I

OF THE MANNER OF LIFE OF ST. FRANCIS WHILST HE
YET WORE THE SECULAR HABIT.

N the city of Assisi there dwelt a man named
Francis, whose memory is in benediction; for
God in His mercy, preventing him with His
divine blessing, vouchsafed to deliver him from the
perils of this present life and filled him abundantly
with the gifts of His heavenly grace. For although he
was brought up in his youth among the vain children
of worldly men in the vanities of the world, and was
employed by his father, as soon as he had acquired
some knowledge of letters, in the pursuit of worldly
gain; yet, by the continual present help of God, he
never suffered himself to be carried away, like the law-
less youths around him, by sensual pleasure, albeit he
was of a gay and joyous spirit; nor, although dwelling
among covetous traders, was he intent upon gain, nor
did he set his heart and hopes on money. For in the
soul of this young man there dwelt, by the gift of God,
a certain innate and natural love of the poor of Christ,
which, growing up with him from his earliest child-
hood, filled his heart with such benignity that, in obedience to the words of the Gospel, he resolved within
himself to give to everyone who should ask of him, and
especially if the petitions were made in the Name of
God. Now it happened one day, when Francis was wholly
engrossed by the tumult of worldly business, that a
poor man asked an alms of him; contrary to his usual
custom he passed him unheeded, and went on his way.

But speedily recollecting himself, he ran after the poor man, charitably relieved his wants, and made a solemn promise to God that, from that day forth, he would never refuse an alms to any that should ask it of him for the love of God. And this promise he faithfully kept till the day of his death, meriting thereby an abundant increase of the grace and love of God. So that he was wont to say, after he had perfectly put on Christ, that even while he still wore the secular habit, he could never hear words expressing the love of God without his heart being deeply moved and affected. And certain it is, that in the sweetness and mildness of his bearing, the gentleness of his manners, his patience and docility—far beyond the ordinary custom of men, the munificence of his bounty, exceeding even the extent of his means—in all these things shone forth the beauty of this young man's soul, clearly betokening the abundant outpouring of the divine blessing reserved for him in days to come.

A certain man of great simplicity dwelt in those days at Assisi, who, by virtue of knowledge divinely infused, whenever he met Francis in the street, would take off his mantle, and spread it upon the ground before him, declaring that he did so because he was a man worthy of all honor and reverence, who should shortly perform great works and marvellous deeds, and was, therefore, to be highly honored and praised by all faithful Christians.

But Francis as yet knew not, neither understood, the great purposes of God towards him; for being by the will of his father engrossed by external affairs, and also by reason of the original corruption of our nature drawn down and depressed by earthly things, he had not learned to contemplate heavenly mysteries, neither did he yet know the sweetness of divine consolation. And, forasmuch as the Lord is wont, by afflictions and tribulations, to open the ears of the spirit, so, by the right hand of the Most High, he was suddenly changed, his body being afflicted with long and severe sufferings, that so his soul might be prepared to receive the unction of the Holy Ghost. Now, when he had recovered his bodily health, going forth one day, as was his wont, in apparel suited to his state, he met a certain soldier of honor and courage, but poor and vilely clad; of whose poverty, feeling a tender and sorrowful compassion, he took off his new clothes and gave them to the poor man-at-arms, thus at once fulfilling two offices of piety, by covering the shame of a noble cavalier and relieving a poor man's penury.

On the following night, when he was asleep, the divine mercy showed him a spacious and beautiful palace filled with arms and military ensigns, all marked with the Cross of Christ, to make known to him that his charitable deed done to the poor soldier for the love of the great King of Heaven should receive an unspeakable reward. And when he asked for whom all these things were reserved, a divine voice answered him that they were for him and for his soldiers.

When Francis awoke, early in the morning, not being yet accustomed to understand and interpret divine mysteries, nor through visible signs to ascend to invisible truths, he thought that this strange vision betokened some great earthly prosperity. Therefore, being still ignorant of the Divine Will, he determined to go into Apulia, there to enter the household of a certain Count of great magnificence and liberality, who dwelt in that country, hoping in his service to acquire military honor and renown, according to what he supposed to be the meaning of the vision. When he had travelled for some days together, he came to a certain city, when the Lord spoke to him in the night with the familiar voice of a friend, saying, "Francis, who can do most for thee—the

Lord or the servant, the rich man or the poor?" And when Francis replied that the Lord and the rich man could do more for him than the poor, "Wherefore, then," said the voice, "dost thou leave the Lord for the servant, and the God of infinite riches for a poor mortal?" Then said Francis, "Lord, what wilt Thou have me to do?" And the Lord answered: "Return home; for the vision which thou hast seen prefigured a spiritual work which thou shalt bring to pass, not by human counsel, but by divine disposition." So, when the day dawned, Francis set forth in great haste towards Assisi, full of joy and confidence; and from that time he awaited in obedience the revelation of the Will of God, and withdrawing from the tumult of worldly affairs, he most devoutly besought the divine clemency to vouchsafe to make manifest to him all that he was to do. And so, by the practice of frequent prayer, the vehement flame of heavenly desires increased daily within him, and already, for the love of his celestial country, he despised all earthly things, as if they existed not; for he knew that he had found the hidden treasure, and like a prudent merchant he considered within himself how to sell all that he had to make it his own. But he knew not yet how he was to purchase it, nor what he was to give for it; only it seemed to be made known to him that the spiritual merchant must begin with the contempt of the world, and that the soldier of Christ must begin by victory over himself.

Now, as he was riding one day over the plain of Assisi he met a leper, whose sudden appearance filled him with fear and horror; but forthwith calling to mind the resolution which he had made to follow after perfection, and remembering that if he would be a soldier of Christ he must first overcome himself, he dismounted from his horse and went to meet the leper, that he might embrace him: and when the poor man stretched out his hand to receive an alms, he kissed it and filled it with money. Having again mounted his horse, he looked around him over the wide and open plain, but nowhere could he see the leper; upon which, being filled with wonder and joy, he began devoutly to give thanks to God, purposing within himself to proceed to still greater things than this.

He sought continually for wild and solitary places, where, with tears and unutterable groans, he poured forth long and fervent prayers, until at last our Lord was pleased to hear him; for being one day engaged in fervent prayer, according to his custom, in a lonely place, he became wholly absorbed in God, when Jesus Christ appeared to him under the form of a Crucifix, at which sight his whole soul seemed to melt away; and so deeply was the memory of Christ's Passion impressed on his heart, that it pierced even to the marrow of his bones. From that hour, whenever he thought upon the Passion of Christ, he could scarcely restrain his tears and sighs; for he then understood (as he made known to some of his familiar friends not long before his death) that these words of the Gospel were addressed to him: "If thou wilt come after Me, deny thyself, and take up thy cross and follow Me." And from that day forth he clothed himself with the spirit of poverty, the sense of humility, and the affection of interior piety. And inasmuch as heretofore he had greatly abhorred the company of lepers, and could not endure even the distant sight of them, now—for the love of Christ crucified, who, according to the Prophet's words, was despised as a leper—he, in contempt of himself, sought out and served lepers with great humility and piety, and aided them in all their necessities. For he often visited them in their houses, giving them bountiful alms, and with affectionate compassion he would kiss their hands and their faces; and he desired to bestow upon poor beggars not only his money, but even himself; oftentimes taking off his own clothes to cover them, tearing or cutting them in pieces for them when he had nothing else to give. With the greatest reverence and piety he was wont to supply the necessities of poor priests, especially by providing them with ornaments for the altar, that so he might at the same time bear his part in the divine worship and provide for the needs of the ministers of God. About this time, he was visiting with great reverence and devotion the holy temple of St. Peter, at Rome; he saw a great multitude of poor surrounding the church door; and partly induced by the love of poverty, partly by the delight which he took in the exercise of works of mercy, he gave his own clothes to the one who seemed most destitute; and putting on the poor man's rags, he remained there all day amidst these poor people, in marvellous joy and gladness of heart, that so despising the glory of the world he might attain to evangelical perfection. He labored with all diligence at the mortification of the flesh, that thus the Cross of Christ, which he bore inwardly in his heart, might be impressed also outwardly on his body. And all these things were done by Francis, this servant of God, before he had taken the religious habit, or separated himself from the conversation of the world.

Chapter II

HROUGHOUT all the time of which we have hitherto spoken, this great servant of God had neither master nor teacher to guide or instruct him, save only Christ our Lord, who, in addition to the gifts already bestowed upon him, was pleased now to visit him with the sweet consolations of His divine grace. For having gone one day into the fields, the better to contemplate and meditate upon heavenly things, he came to the church of St. Damian, which, from its great antiquity, was fast falling into decay, and, by the inspiration of the Spirit of God, he went in thither to pray. As he lay prostrate before a Crucifix he was filled with great spiritual consolation, and gazing with tearful eyes upon the holy Cross of the Lord, he heard with his bodily ears a voice from the Crucifix, which said thrice to him: "Francis, go and build up My house, which, as thou seest, is falling into ruin." Then Francis, trembling, and full of fear, being in the church alone, wondered at the sound of that marvellous voice, and as his heart received the meaning and power of the divine words he fell into a great ecstasy. When he had recovered his senses, and came to himself, he prepared to obey, and set himself at once to fulfill the command which he had received to repair the material church, although the principal intention of these words referred to that Church which Christ has purchased and built up with His precious Blood,

7

as the Holy Spirit afterwards revealed to him, and as he afterwards made known to the friars.

He arose, therefore, and fortifying himself with the Sign of the Cross, he took out of his house a number of pieces of cloth, with which he went in all haste to the city of Foligno, where he sold all the merchandise which he had brought with him, and the horse also which had carried it, and so the happy merchant returned to Assisi, and reverently entering the church which had been committed to his care, he found there a poor priest, to whom, with due reverence, he offered all his goods for the repair of that church, and for the necessities and use of the poor, humbly beseeching him to suffer him to dwell with him there for awhile.

The priest was well content that he should remain there, but for fear of his father and mother he refused the proffered money. Francis, however, who cared not for anything that might befall him, threw down all the money on a ledge of a window, as if it had been so much dust, and so left it in contempt.

Now when the servant of God had dwelt some days with this priest, his father, coming to hear of it, hastened in great anger to the church. Francis being yet a novice in the service of Christ, hearing the loud threats of his persecutors, and expecting their approach, resolved to give place to wrath, and hid himself for some days in a very secret place, beseeching the Lord continually, with many tears, to deliver his soul from the hands of those who persecuted him, that so he might accomplish the pious design with which He had inspired him. Then, being filled with exceeding joy, he began to reproach himself with his fearfulness and faintness of heart, and leaving his retreat, and casting away all fear, he made his way to Assisi, where, when the citizens saw him, pale and meagre in countenance, and changed in mind and character, many of them judged that he was out of his senses, and began to throw stones and mud at him and to cry after him as a madman. But the good servant of God, unmoved by all these insults, went on his way as if he heard them not. These cries soon reached the ears of his father, who ran to the spot, not to deliver him, but rather to oppress him more cruelly: for seizing him without mercy, he dragged him to his house, reproaching and tormenting him with words, blows and bonds. But he who had now become more prompt and valiant in the service of his Lord, called to mind those words of the Gospel: "Blessed are they who are persecuted for justice' sake, for theirs is the kingdom of heaven."

Not long afterwards his father was compelled by the affairs of his merchandise to leave Assisi, when his mother, disapproving her husband's treatment of Francis, and seeing that there was no hope of shaking the invincible constancy of her son, freed him from his bonds and gave him liberty to go whithersoever he would. And so, returning thanks to Almighty God, he returned to St. Damian's.

When his father came home and found that he was gone, he severely reproved his wife, and went in great anger to seek him, being minded, if he could not bring him home, to drive him altogether out of the country. But Francis, in the strength of God, went forth of his own accord to meet his furious father, declaring that he feared neither his blows nor his chains, and protesting that he was ready to bear every suffering which might await him for the Name of Christ.

The father, seeing that his son could not be moved from his purpose, turned his thoughts next to the recovery of his money. Having found this at last lying, as has been said, on a window-sill, his anger was in some measure appeased by the recovery of the money, which satisfied the thirst of his avarice.

And now his father according to the flesh, having despoiled him of his money, brought this son (no longer his, but the child of divine grace) before the Bishop of Assisi, to compel him to renounce in his hands all his inheritance, and whatsoever he had received from him, which this true lover of poverty was most ready and willing to do. As soon, therefore, as he came into the Bishop's presence, without a moment's delay, neither waiting for his father's demand nor uttering a word himself, he laid aside all his clothes, and gave them back to his father. Then it was seen, that under his fair and costly garments the holy man wore a hard and rough hair-shirt. With marvellous fervor he then turned to his father, and spoke thus to him in the presence of all: "Until this hour I have called thee my father on earth; from henceforth, I may say confidently, *my Father Who art in Heaven,* in Whose hands I have laid up all my treasures, all my trust, and all my hope."

When the Bishop, who was a man of great virtue and piety, heard this, he marvelled at the exceeding fervor of the holy man of God, and rising from his seat, he embraced him with many tears, covering him with his mantle, and he commanded his servants to bring some garment wherewith to clothe him. There was brought to him a poor mantle, belonging to a certain laborer of the Bishop, which Francis received with exceeding joy; and with a piece of chalk, which he found lying there, he made the Sign of the Cross upon it, as a garment well befitting a poor half-naked man, crucified to the world.

And thus did this most faithful servant of the great King of Heaven and earth strip himself of all things, that so he might follow the Lord, Whom he so truly loved, Who died naked on the Cross for him; and thus did he arm himself with the Sign of the Cross, committing his soul to that sacred wood of our salvation, to escape thereby from the fearful shipwreck of the world.

From that day forth this great despiser of the world, being freed from all the bonds of worldly cupidity, went forth from the city to a secret and solitary place, where, alone and in silence, he waited the revelation of the Divine Will.

Now it came to pass, that as Francis, the servant of God, was singing the praises of the Lord with great joy and gladness, certain robbers fell upon him and fiercely questioned him, asking him who he was. And when he answered them in truly prophetic words: "I am the herald of the great King of Heaven," the robbers fell upon him with great fury, and having loaded him with blows, they cast him into a ditch filled with snow, saying: "Lie there, thou herald of nothing, who callest thyself the herald of God." When they had departed, Francis arose, and, full of exceeding joy, went through the forest, singing with a loud voice the praises of his Creator; and having come to a neighboring monastery, he there asked an alms as a poor man, and as such he received it, for it was given to him as to a vile and unknown person.

From thence he came to Gubbio, where he was recognized by one of his own friends, who received him into his house, and gave him a poor old tunic, with which he clothed himself, as in deed and in truth the poor servant of God.

Afterwards, in his deep love of humility, he went among the lepers and remained with them, serving them diligently for the love of God. He washed their feet, bound up their wounds, pressing out the corrupt matter, and then washing and cleansing them. And having done this he kissed their wounds with great and marvellous devotion, as one who in brief space was to become an evangelical physician, and true healer of souls. Nay, such power was bestowed upon him by the Lord, that he obtained a wonderful gift to cure, not corporal only, but spiritual diseases. And amongst many such marvellous deeds we will relate one, the fame whereof was spread throughout all that country.

There was a certain man at Spoleto who was tormented and consumed by a malignant disease, which had eaten away his mouth and jaw, nor could any remedy be found for it. It so befell, that he went to Rome to beseech the Prince of the Apostles and many other Saints by their merits to obtain for him favor from God. On his return from his pilgrimage, he happened to meet with the man of God. And desiring, for the great devotion which he bore him, to kiss his feet, the humble Francis, who could not suffer it, kissed his diseased and loathsome mouth. Now, no sooner had this true servant of God and of the lepers with such marvellous pity touched that horrible wound with his holy mouth, than the disease utterly disappeared, and the sick man recovered his health.

Assuredly I know not which of these two things is most worthy of admiration, the profound humility of that kiss, or the marvellous power which wrought so stupendous a miracle.

Francis, being thus established in the humility of Christ, called to mind the obedience laid upon him by the voice from the Crucifix, to rebuild the church of St. Damian; and being perfect in his obedience, he returned to Assisi, that, if in no other way, he might by begging obtain means to fulfill the divine command. And therefore despising for the love of the poor crucified Jesus the shame of going to beg of those amongst whom he had once lived in honor and wealth, he, moreover, laid heavy burdens upon his body, already wasted with fasting, carrying great stones on his own shoulders for the building of the church.

When he had rebuilt the aforesaid church by the

help of the Lord and the devotion of his fellow-citizens, who largely assisted him—lest, having finished this labor, he should begin to grow slothful, he set to work to repair the church of St. Peter, a little farther from the city, for the special devotion which, in the sincere purity of his faith, he bore to the Prince of the Apostles.

When St. Peter's church was finished, he came to a place called Portiuncula, where was a church built in ancient times to the honor of the Blessed Virgin Mother of God, and under her invocation, but which had been deserted, and which, for want of care, was now falling into decay. The holy man, beholding it thus desolate, resolved, out of his fervent devotion to the Queen of the world, to remain there, in order to repair and restore it. And while he abode there, he received frequent angelical visitations in accordance with the name of the church, which was *St. Mary of the Angels*. Here, therefore, he resolved to remain, because of his reverence to the Angels, and, above all, because of the exceeding love which he bore to the Mother of Christ. This place was loved by the holy man above all places in the world, for here, in great humility, he began his spiritual life; here he grew in virtue; here he attained his happy and perfect end; and this, at the hour of his death, he commended to his brethren as a spot most dear to the Blessed Virgin. It was at this place that a certain very devout friar beheld a vision well worthy to be related; he saw a multitude of men, who were all blind, kneeling round this church, with their faces and hands raised to heaven, and with many tears crying to God to have mercy on them. And behold there appeared a great glory in Heaven shining over them all, which gave light and salvation to each. This is the place in which, by divine revelation, St. Francis instituted the Order of the Friars Minor. For, by

the direction of Divine Providence, by which the servant of Christ was guided in all things, he built three
material churches before he began to preach the
Gospel, and instituted that Order, that thus, not only
he might ascend from things sensible to things intel-
lectual, from the less to the greater, but also that the
visible work might mysteriously prefigure that which
was hereafter to be brought to pass. For after the
similitude of the three churches repaired by the holy
man, according to the rule and doctrine revealed to
him, so was the Church of Christ restored by the vic-
tories of three kinds of spiritual warriors, as we see
fulfilled at this day.

Chapter III

OF THE INSTITUTION OF THE ORDER, AND THE
APPROBATION OF THE RULE OF ST. FRANCIS.

RANCIS, the servant of God, abode thus for some time in the church of the Virgin Mother of God, pouring forth continual prayers to her who had conceived the *Word, full of grace and truth,* that she would vouchsafe to be his advocate; and now, by the merits of that Mother of Mercy, he conceived and brought forth the spirit of evangelical truth. For, as he was one day devoutly hearing the Mass of the Apostles, the Gospel was read wherein is contained the Mission of Christ to His Apostles, and the rule of evangelical life which He gave them when he sent them out to preach; bidding them take neither gold, nor silver, nor money in their purse; nor to carry a scrip; nor to have two tunics, nor shoes, nor staff.

Now when this true lover of Apostolical poverty heard these words, he was filled with inconceivable joy. "This," he said within himself, "is what I above all things desire. That is what my whole heart craves." And so saying, he cast off the shoes from his feet, laid aside the staff which he bore, and throwing away his purse and all that he possessed, he clad himself in a single tunic, and, instead of the belt which he wore, he girded himself with a cord, casting away all worldly cares, and giving his whole heart to carry out the command which he had heard, and to shape his life in all things according to the strict rule of Apostolical poverty. From this day forward the man of God began, by divine inspiration, to strive after evangelical perfection, and to invite all men to holy penance. And because there was no vanity or levity in his words, but they were grave and efficacious, and full of the power of the Holy Ghost, they pierced even to the depths of men's hearts, filling all that heard him with great amazement. And in all his discourses he proclaimed peace, saluting the people at the beginning of all his sermons with these words: "God give you His peace;" having learned this salutation (as he afterwards declared) by divine revelation.

And so, according to his prophetic words (being filled also with the prophetical spirit), he proclaimed peace, he preached peace, and by his salutary admonitions he reconciled to Him, Who is the true Peace, many who, being at enmity with Christ, were far from the way of salvation.

Many having become thus acquainted with the truth and simplicity of the holy man's teaching, and with the sanctity of his life, began, after his example, to follow after penance; and, forsaking all earthly things, they assumed his habit, and became companions of his life.

The first of these was a holy man named Bernard, who, having been made a partaker of the divine vocation, deserves to be called the first-born son of this holy Father, by priority of time, and no less by pre-eminence of sanctity.

This man, then, having heard of the sanctity of Francis, the servant of Christ, and desiring, after his example, perfectly to despise the world, asked counsel of him how he should carry his purpose into effect, which, when the servant of God had heard, he was filled with spiritual consolation at the words of this his first-born son. "This counsel," said he, "must be asked of God." Therefore early in the morning they entered the church of St. Nicolas, and having prayed to God, Francis, who was most devout to the Most Holy Trinity, thrice opened the book of the Gospels, beseeching our Lord that, by three several testimonies, He would be pleased to confirm the holy purpose of Bernard. The first time he opened the book they came upon this passage: "If thou wilt be perfect, go and sell all that thou hast and give to the poor." The second time they read: "Take nothing for your journey." And the third time: "He who will come after Me, let him deny himself, and take up his cross and follow Me." "This," said the holy man, "is our life and our rule, and the life and the rule of all those who would join our company; if, then, thou wilt be perfect, go and do what thou hast heard." Not long afterwards, five others having been called by the same Spirit, the number of the sons of St. Francis amounted to six, amongst whom he who held the third place was the holy Father Giles, a man assuredly full of God, and worthy of all remembrance; for he became afterwards illustrious by the exercise of many sublime virtues, even as the servant of God had foretold of him; so that, although he was simple and unlearned, he was, nevertheless, exalted to a sublime degree of heavenly contemplation; for being for a long space of time continually intent upon heavenly things, he was by frequent ecstasies so rapt in God (as I have often seen with mine own eyes) that he might be rather said to live amongst men the life of an Angel than of a man.

About the same time, the Lord vouchsafed a very remarkable vision to a certain priest named Sylvester, of the city of Assisi, a man of pious, holy life. When he beheld the manner of life led by Francis and his friars, viewing it only with the eyes of human prudence, he felt an abhorrence of it; and lest he should be led astray by rash judgment, the following vision was vouchsafed to him by our Lord. He saw in a dream the whole city of Assisi encompassed by a great and terrible dragon, which threatened the whole place with destruction.

Then, from the mouth of Francis, there seemed to issue a great cross of gold, the top of which touched heaven, and the two arms of which stretched to the extremities of the world. Before its brightness the terrible dragon fled away. Having seen this vision three times, he judged it to be a divine oracle, and related it in order to the holy man and his friars; and not long afterwards he left the world, and followed the footsteps of Christ so closely as to prove by his life in religion the truth of this vision which he had seen in the world.

When Francis, the man of God, heard of this vision, he was not lifted up with pride and vain-glory, but acknowledging the goodness of God in all His benefits, he was filled with fresh courage to withstand the arts of the old serpent, and to preach the glory of the Cross of Christ.

Now, having withdrawn one day to a certain solitary place, to mourn over his past life in bitterness of heart, he was filled by the Holy Ghost with extraordinary gladness, being assured of the full remission of all his sins. Being thus rapt in ecstasy, and, as it were, absorbed in a marvellous light of contemplation, his mind was opened to see what should befall him and his sons in days to come. Then, returning to his brethren, he said: "Be comforted, my dearest children, and rejoice in the Lord, and be not troubled because you are so few, nor affrighted by reason of your simplicity, for the Lord has truly shown me that God will make us increase to a great multitude, and will pour forth the grace of His benediction upon us."

At the same time another good man entered the religion of Francis, so that his blessed family now numbered seven. Then the holy Father called all his sons to him, and having spoken many things to them concerning the kingdom of God, the denial of their own will, and the mortification of the flesh, he made known to them his purpose of sending them into the four quarters of the world; for now the poor and barren simplicity of the holy Father having brought forth these seven sons, he desired that, with the voice of penance, they should bring forth the whole company of the faithful to Christ his Lord. "Go," said our sweet Father to his children, "proclaim peace to men, preach penance for the remission of sins. Be patient in tribulation, watchful in prayer, strong in labor, moderate in speech, grave in conversation, thankful for benefits; for if you shall observe all these things, an eternal kingdom is prepared for you." And when they heard these words they prostrated themselves humbly before the servant of God, receiving with gladness of heart the command of holy obedience. And after this he said singly to each, "Cast thy care upon the Lord, and He will nourish thee." And these words he was accustomed to say to every brother to whom he gave an obedience. Then, knowing that he was given as an example to others, and that he should first do that which he taught them to do, he went with one companion towards one part of the world; sending the other six, two and two, into the three other parts; thus dividing the world after the manner of a Cross.

After a little time, this loving Father desired to have his children with him again, and being unable to assemble them himself, he prayed to Him Who gathers together the dispersed of Israel, to bring them all together in one place. And so it came to pass that, without human vocation, the divine clemency brought them marvelously in an incredibly short space of time into the place where he was; and now four other good and holy men were added to their number, which thus amounted to twelve.

The servant of Christ, seeing that the number of his friars was gradually increasing, wrote for himself and for them a rule and form of life, laying as its immovable foundation the observance of the holy Gospel, and adding a few other things which he thought necessary for uniformity of life. Desiring that the things which he had written should be approved by the supreme Pontiff, he determined (depending only on the divine direction) to go with his simple company to the Throne of the Apostle. God beheld from Heaven the desire of His servant, and lest the souls of his companions should be affrighted by the consideration of their own simplicity, He strengthened the heart of the holy man by the following vision. It seemed to him that he was travelling along a certain road, by the side of which there grew a lofty tree, to which he drew near, and as he stood under its shadow, marvelling at its height, he was suddenly lifted up by the divine power, until he touched the top of the tree, which bowed itself towards him. Now the man of God understood, by the Divine Spirit Who dwelt in him, that this vision signified the condescension of the sublime dignity of the Apostolic See to his desire; and so, being full of spiritual joy, he comforted his brethren in the Lord, and set forth with them on his journey.

When they were come to the Roman Court, and brought into the presence of the Sovereign Pontiff, the Vicar of Christ was walking on a terrace of the Lateran, in deep and serious meditation, and seeing the servant of Christ to be an unknown stranger, he indignantly repulsed him.

Francis retired with all humility, and on the following night the Sovereign Pontiff received a revelation from God. He saw a palm-tree gradually grow up at his feet until it reached a goodly stature, and as he gazed upon it, wondering what the vision might mean, a divine illumination impressed on the mind of the Vicar of Christ that this palm-tree signified the poor man whom he had driven that day from his presence.

The next morning, therefore, he sent his servants through the city to seek for this poor man, whom they found in the hospital of St. Antony, hard by the Lateran Palace. When he was brought into the presence of the Sovereign Pontiff, Francis made known his desire, praying humbly and earnestly for the approbation of his rule. Our Lord, Innocent III, who was then the Vicar of Christ, and a man illustrious for his wisdom, admiring the purity and simplicity of heart which he beheld in the man of God, his great constancy of purpose, and the exceeding fervor of his holy will, lovingly embraced Christ's poor man, being ready, with all willingness, to grant his pious petition. Yet he delayed to do so for awhile, because it seemed to some of the cardinals that the rule was a novelty, and beyond human strength to observe.

Now, there was among the cardinals a venerable man named John of St. Paul, Bishop of Sabina, a lover of all sanctity, and the benefactor of the poor of Christ. He, being enlightened by the Holy Ghost, spoke thus to the Sovereign Pontiff and to his brethren: "If we refuse this poor man's petition, as a novelty too hard to be observed, whereas he only begs for the confirmation of the evangelical way of life, let us take heed lest we offend against the Gospel of Christ. For, if any man shall say that the observance and the vow of evangelical perfection contain anything irrational or impossible to be observed, he is convicted of blasphemy against Christ, the Author of the Gospel." When the successor of the Apostle Peter had heard these words, he said: "My son, pray to Christ, our Lord, that He would make known His Will to us by thy mouth, for, when we shall have more certain knowledge, we shall be able with greater security to fulfill thy pious desires." The servant of Almighty God betook himself, therefore, to devout prayer, that he might be directed what to say to the Holy Father, and that the Holy Father might be moved favorably to receive his words. He came, then, again to the Vicar of Christ, and spoke to him the following parable: "There was," said Francis, "a rich and mighty king, who took to wife a poor but very beautiful woman, in whom he greatly delighted, and by whom he had children who bore the image of their father, and whom, by God's command, the king brought up in his own palace, and fed at his royal table." And he added this interpretation: "There is no fear," said he, "that the children and heirs of the Eternal King should perish with hunger, who by the power of the Holy Ghost have been born of a poor mother, and bear the image of Christ the King, being born by the spirit of poverty, in a religion of poverty. If, therefore, the King of Heaven has promised His followers an eternal kingdom, how much rather will He provide them with those things which He is wont to impart indifferently to the evil and the good?" Now, when the Vicar of Christ had diligently attended to this parable and its interpretation, he marvelled greatly, and acknowledged that, without doubt, Christ had spoken by the mouth of that man.

Another vision which was vouchsafed to him about this time, concerning the things which St. Francis was to accomplish, confirmed the revelation which he had now received from the Holy Ghost. He saw in a dream the Lateran Basilica, now falling into ruin, supported by the shoulders of a poor, despised, and feeble man. "Truly," said he, "this is he who by his works and his teaching shall sustain the Church of Christ." Hence, he was filled with a great and special devotion and love for the servant of God. He granted all his petitions, and promised to grant him still greater things. He approved the rule, gave him a mission to preach penance, and granted to all the lay brothers in the company of the servant of God to wear a tonsure smaller than that worn by priests, and freely to preach the Word of God.

Chapter IV

FTER these things, Francis, being full of faith in divine grace, and the approbation of the Apostolic See, went his way to the Valley of Spoleto, there to preach the Gospel, and to fulfill the evangelical precepts. And on his way he conferred with his companions as to how they should perfectly observe the rule which they had received, walking before God in all holiness and justice, that so they might make continual progress themselves, and give good example to others. And as they discoursed at length upon these matters, they perceived not that the time of their collation was passed. And so, being weary with their long journey, and faint with hunger, they came to a solitary place, where there were no means of obtaining necessary food; but the Providence of God was present with them. For a man suddenly appeared before them, carrying a loaf in his hand, which he gave to Christ's poor men, and immediately disappeared; so that they knew not whence he came, nor whither he went. The poor friars, therefore, knowing by this sign that God's help would never fail them so long as they should be in company with the holy man, were strengthened rather by the gift of the divine bounty than by the corporal food, and were, moreover, filled with divine consolation, so that they made a firm and irrevocable resolution that neither for hunger nor suffering of any kind would they break the promise they had plighted to holy poverty.

Having made this firm resolve, they returned into the Valley of Spoleto, considering within themselves whether they should live amongst men, or retire to some solitary place. But Francis, the servant of Christ, trusting not to his own industry to discover the Will of God, sought for it by intense and earnest prayer. And it was made known to him by divine revelation that he was sent by God to win back to Christ the souls which the devil was seeking to carry away. He therefore determined to live not only for himself but for the good of all; being moved thereto by the example of Him Who vouchsafed to die for all. Therefore the man of God gathered his companions together, and dwelt with them in a deserted hut, near the city of Assisi, in which, according to the rule of holy poverty, they lived in much labor and necessity, caring rather to satisfy themselves with the bread of tears than with delicate food. Here they passed their time in continual prayer, and that rather mental than vocal, for they had no ecclesiastical books from which they might chant their canonical hours. But instead of such books they contemplated the Cross of Christ continually, day and night, after the example of their Father, and being instructed by the discourses which he addressed to them continually concerning the Cross of Christ. For when the brethren asked him to teach them to pray, he said: "When you pray, say the *Pater Noster*, and *We adore Thee, O Christ, in all Thy churches which are in all the world, and we bless Thee because by Thy holy Cross Thou hast redeemed the world.*" He taught them also that they should praise God in all things and by all creatures, and that they should pay especial honors to priests, and that they should hold the truth of the faith according to what the holy Roman Church holds and teaches, and firmly believe and simply confess it.

The friars observed their holy Father's teaching in all things; and, whenever they saw a church or a Cross, though it were a long way off, they humbly prostrated themselves, and said the form of prayer which he had given them. Now, while the brethren abode in the place aforesaid, the holy man went on a certain Saturday into the city of Assisi, for he was to preach on the Sunday morning, as was his custom, in the Cathedral Church. And being thus absent in body from his children, and engaged in devout prayer to God (as was his custom throughout the night), in a certain hut in the canons' garden, about midnight, whilst some of the brethren were asleep, and others watching in prayer, a chariot of fire, of marvellous splendor, was seen to enter the door, and thrice to pass hither and thither through the house; and over the chariot was seen a globe of dazzling light, like to the glory of the sun, which turned the night into day. The watchers were amazed, the sleepers aroused and affrighted; for that light illuminated the spirit no less than the body, and by its marvellous power the conscience of each was laid bare to his brethren. Now all, with one consent, understood (each beholding the heart of the other) that their holy Father, being absent in body, was present in spirit, and was thus divinely manifested to them, transfigured into that form of heavenly light, burning with the fire of celestial virtue, that they, as true Israelites, might follow after him, who, like another Elias, was made by God both the chariot and the charioteer. They believed also that He had opened the eyes of these simple men, at the prayer of Francis, to see the wonderful works of God, as He opened the eyes of the sons of the prophets to behold the mountain full of horsemen and fiery chariots around Elias. Now, when the holy man returned to his brethren, he began to discover the secrets of their consciences, and comforted them concerning this marvellous vision, foretelling also many things which should come to pass for the good of his Order. And as he thus revealed to them many things transcending human knowledge, the brethren knew that the Spirit of the Lord rested in all His plenitude upon His servant Francis, and that they would be most assuredly safe and blessed in following his life and teaching. After these things, Francis, the pastor of this little flock, under the guidance of divine grace, led his twelve brethren to St. Mary of the Portiuncula, that the Order of the Friars Minor, which had been born there by the merits of the Mother of God, might there also by her aid receive its increase. And while he abode there, he went about all the cities and towns preaching the Gospel, not with the words of human wisdom, but in the power of the Spirit, announcing the kingdom of God. And, beholding him as a man of another world, having his eyes and his heart always fixed on heaven, many were drawn to follow him thither. And thenceforward Christ's vine began to bring forth the sweet flowers of the Lord, and abundant fruits of sweetness, honor, and virtue. And by the fervor of his preaching, many of both sexes, who served God in conjugal purity, were enkindled to ask for a rule of life from the holy man, and to bind themselves by new bonds of penance, who, living after this manner, received from the servant of God the name of Brethren and Sisters of the Third Order of Penance. This state and order admitted all manner of persons, laymen and clerics, virgins and married persons, men and women; and God has testified His acceptance of the same by many miracles wrought by its members. Many virgins were also called to a life of perpetual chastity, amongst whom was Clare, that virgin most dear to God, the first flower amongst them all, who, like a sweet spring blossom, diffused a fragrant odor around her, and shone like a brilliant star in the Church of God. She who is now glorified in Heaven, and worthily venerated by the Church on earth, was the daughter in Christ of the holy Father Francis, the poor servant of God, and the mother of the *Poor Ladies* (now called Poor Clares).

Many being thus not only pierced with compunction, but inflamed with a desire for the perfection of Christ, followed in the footsteps of Francis, despising all the vanities of the world, so that the number of his followers, marvelously increasing from day to day, soon reached the limits of the world: for holy poverty, which they took with them as their only procuratrix, made them prompt in obedience, strong to labor, and swift of foot. And because they possessed nothing earthly, and feared to lose nothing earthly, they were secure in all places; troubled by no fears, distracted by no cares, they lived without trouble of mind, waited without solicitude for the coming day, or the night's lodging. Many sufferings and insults were inflicted upon them in divers parts of the world, as on men unknown, vile, and of no account; but the love of the Gospel of Christ had given them so much patience, that they sought rather to be where they might endure persecution in the body, than where (their sanctity being known) they might receive honor and favor from the world. And from this their penury they reaped exceeding abundance, according to the counsel of the wise man, who chose less rather than more.

Now it came to pass that some of the brethren went into an infidel country, and a certain Saracen, moved with pity, offered them money to buy necessary food; and when they refused it, the man marvelled greatly, seeing how poor they were. But when he understood that, having become poor for the love of God, they refused to possess anything, he was so moved with admiration that he offered to minister to them, and to provide for all their necessities, so long as he should have anything in his possession. Oh, inestimable value of poverty! By whose marvellous power the fierceness of this barbarian was turned into such sweet compassion. Shameful and horrible is it to see a Christian man trample upon that precious pearl, which was thus venerated even by a Saracen.

About this time, a certain religious man, of the Order of the Crucified Friars, Moricus by name—who had been languishing for a long time in a hospital near Assisi, under a grievous sickness, and was now judged by the physicians to be nigh to death—sent a messenger to the holy man, to beseech him earnestly to intercede for him with the Lord. And the holy Father, benignly consenting to his request, took some pieces of bread, and having steeped them in the oil which burned before an image of the Blessed Virgin, sent it by the hands of his friars to the sick man, saying, "Take this medicine to our dear brother, Moricus, that, by the power of Christ, he may not only fully recover his health, but may be strengthened to become a valiant warrior, and stedfastly cleave to our army." No sooner, then, had the sick man tasted the antidote prepared for him by the inspiration of the Holy Ghost, than he arose, having obtained from God such perfect health and vigor both of mind and body, that he soon afterwards entered the religion of the holy man, wearing only a single tunic, under which, for a long time, he wore a shirt of mail. He fed continually upon uncooked herbs, vegetables, and fruit—for a long space of time tasting neither bread nor wine; and yet he preserved his health and strength under the hardships of this way of life.

The merits and virtues of these little ones of Christ thus daily increasing, the odor of their good report was spread throughout all that country, and many were drawn to the presence of the holy Father from divers parts of the world; amongst whom came a certain man, ingenious in the composition of secular verses, who had been crowned by the Emperor, and was hence called king of poesy. He came to seek the holy man who despised all earthly things, and he found him in the city of San Severino, preaching in a monastery, the hand of God being upon him. And as he preached, it seemed that the Cross of Christ was traced upon his body by two flaming swords, placed over each other in the form of a Cross, one of which reached from his head to his feet, and the other across his breast from one hand to the other. Now the minstrel knew not the countenance of the servant of Christ, but by that miracle he recognized him at once, and determined to change his life; for, being pierced by the power of his words, and, as it were, transfixed by the sword of the Spirit which issued from his mouth, he cast away all the pomps and vanities of the world and embraced the profession of the blessed Father. Wherefore the holy man, seeing that he was converted from the perturbations of the world to the perfect peace of Christ, gave him the name of Brother Pacificus. This man, being afterwards filled with all sanctity before he was made Minister-General in France (he was the first to fill that office), was counted worthy, on another occasion, to see the great Sign of the Cross, in a distinct variety of colors, adorn the forehead of St. Francis. For the holy man had a great veneration for that sacred sign, often discoursed in its praise, and always inscribed it upon all the letters which he wrote with his own hand; as if it had been all his care (according to the words of the prophet) to sign with that sign of *Tau* the foreheads of all those who, in weeping and mourning, are truly converted to Christ.

In process of time, the number of the friars being greatly multiplied, their watchful pastor assembled them all in general chapter in the holy place of St. Mary of the Portiuncula; that by divine distribution, each should receive his portion from obedience, according to their poverty. Now, although there was a want there of things necessary to life, and although more than five thousand friars were gathered together at one time in that place, nevertheless, by the divine clemency, there was food sufficient for all, and they were all full of corporal health and spiritual joy. But as to the provincial chapter, although he could not be present with them in the body, yet by his solicitude for their good government, his earnest prayers and effectual benediction, he was always present with them in spirit; and oftentimes also, by the marvellous power of God, he even appeared visibly among them. For when the illustrious preacher and glorious Confessor, Antony, who is now with Christ, was preaching to the brethren in the chapel at Arles on the title upon the Cross— "Jesus of Nazareth, the King of the Jews"—a certain friar of approved virtue named Monaldus, casting his eyes by divine inspiration upon the door of the chapter-house, beheld, with his bodily eyes, the blessed Francis raised in the air, blessing the brethren, with his hands outstretched in the form of a Cross. And the brethren were at the same time filled with such true and unwonted consolation, that they were assured, by the testimony of the Spirit, that the holy man was truly present with them. And not long afterwards this truth was certified, not only by these evident signs, but by the words of the holy Father himself. And it is surely to be believed that the power of Almighty God, by which the holy Bishop St. Ambrose was present at the burial of the glorious St. Martin, to do honor to that holy Pontiff, also caused His servant Francis to be present at the preaching of His true herald Antony, that he might thus bear testimony to the truth of his words, especially concerning the Cross of Christ, of which he was the true minister and standard-bearer. Now, seeing that the Order and form of life already approved by Pope Innocent was greatly enlarged and increased, Francis desired, in obedience to the divine revelation, to procure its perpetual confirmation from his successor, Honorius. It seemed to him one night, in a vision, that he was gathering from the ground some very small morsels of bread; and, as he was about to distribute them amongst a number of friars who were famishing round him, and doubting how he could distribute such small pieces, fearing lest they should fall from his hands, a voice from Heaven said to him, "Francis, make one Host of all these pieces, and give to as many as desire to receive." And when he had done this, all those who received that Host without devotion, or despised the offered Gift, were immediately struck with leprosy, and so visibly distinguished from the rest. In the morning, the holy man related the vision to his companions, grieving that he could not understand the mystery signified thereby. On the following day, as he persevered in prayer, he again heard the same voice from Heaven: "Francis," it said, "the crumbs of bread which thou didst see last night are the words of the Gospel, the Host is the rule, the leprosy is sin." Then he set himself to bring into a shorter form the words of the Gospel, which at that time were scattered somewhat diffusely through the rule, which was now to be confirmed according to the vision which he had seen. He took with him two friars as his companions; and being guided by the Holy Ghost, he went to a mountain, where he fasted upon bread and water; and there he caused the rule to be written, according to what the Divine Spirit suggested to him while he prayed. And this rule, when he came down from the mountain, he committed to the keeping of his Vicar, who, after a few days had elapsed, declared that he had carelessly lost it. Once more, therefore, the holy man returned to that solitary place, and there he re-wrote the rule as at the first, as he had received the words from the mouth of God. And by the above-named Pope Honorius, in the eighth year of his Pontificate, it was confirmed; and to enforce on the brethren the more fervent observance of that rule, he was accustomed to say that there was therein nothing of his own industry or device, but that he wrote all things as they were revealed to him by God.

That this truth might be certified by the testimony of God, not many days afterwards the Stigmata of the Lord Jesus were impressed upon his body by the finger of the living God—the bull, as it were, of Christ, the Supreme Pontiff, in confirmation of the rule, and in commendation of its Author, as, after the narration of his virtues, shall be related in its place.

Chapter V

OF THE AUSTERITY OF HIS LIFE, AND HOW ALL
CREATURES GAVE HIM JOY AND CONSOLATION.

OW when Francis, the servant of God, saw that many were excited and encouraged by his example to take up the Cross of Christ, and to follow him as a brave leader of Christ's army, he himself grew still more fervent in his endeavor to attain the palm of victory by the practice of every sublime virtue. And considering those words of the Apostle, "They who are Christ's have crucified the flesh with its concupiscences," to clothe his body in the strong armor of the Cross, he began to exercise such severe discipline over all his sensual appetites, that he hardly took such food as was necessary for the support of nature. For he said that it was hard to satisfy the necessities of the body without indulging the inclinations of the senses. Therefore he rarely ate any food which had been cooked with fire; and when he did so, he mixed so much water therewith as to render it insipid. And what shall I say of his drinking?—for he would hardly allow himself cold water enough to slake the burning thirst with which he was oftentimes tormented.

He continually discovered new ways of exercising abstinence, increasing daily in its exercise; and even when he had attained the summit of perfection he still endeavored, as if only a beginner, to punish, by fresh macerations, the rebellion of the flesh. Nevertheless, when he went abroad, he conformed himself (according to the words of the Gospel) to the manner of life of those with whom he abode, eating what was set before him; but when he returned home, he resumed the practice of his rule of rigid abstinence. So that, being austere to himself, and gentle to his neighbor, and thus subject in all things to the Gospel of Christ, he gave edification in all things, whether by eating or abstaining. The bare earth was the ordinary bed of his wearied body, and he often slept sitting, leaning his head against a stone, or a block of wood, and being covered only with one poor tunic. Thus he served the Lord in cold and nakedness.

Being once asked how, in that poor clothing, he could endure the severity of the winter's cold, he made answer, in fervor of spirit, "If we burn within with a fervent desire for our heavenly country, easy it is to endure this exterior cold." He abhorred soft and delicate clothing and loved that which was coarse and rough, saying that our Lord praised John the Baptist for wearing such. If a tunic were given him somewhat softer than usual, he would make the inside rough with little cords; for he said that, according to the word of truth, soft raiment is to be sought for in the palaces of princes; and that experience assuredly teaches that the devils are afraid of rough clothing, but are encouraged to tempt those who indulge in softness and delicacy. One night, accordingly, when, on account of a pain in his head and eyes, a feather pillow had been placed under his head, the devil entered into it, and troubled him in many ways, even till the hour of matins, hindering from prayer, until he called his companion, and begged him to carry the pillow, and the devil with it, far from the cell. No sooner had the brother gone out with the pillow than he lost all the power and use of his limbs, until, at the prayer of the holy Father, who saw it in spirit, his wonted strength of mind and body was fully restored to him.

Now the holy man Francis watched most diligently over himself, becoming ever more and more rigid in his care of the purity both of the interior and exterior man; for which cause, in the beginning of his conversion, he would often plunge in winter-time into a pit of ice and snow, that he might more perfectly subdue his domestic enemy, and preserve the white garment of his purity from the fire of temptation. For he said that it was beyond comparison easier for a spiritual man to endure the utmost extremity of cold in his body, than the slightest spark of sinful passion in his soul. As he was one night praying in his cell, at the hermitage of Sartiano, the old enemy called him thrice, saying: "Francis, Francis, Francis!" And when Francis asked him what he sought, he answered, deceitfully: "There is no sinner in the world, who, if he be converted, shall not obtain pardon of God. But he who shall destroy himself by excessive penance shall obtain no mercy for all eternity." The man of God knew by revelation the deceit of the enemy, who thus sought to delude him into tepidity, as was proved by the event.

For, by the breath of that infernal enemy, which is wont to kindle the fire of concupiscence, he was assailed by a violent temptation. Then this holy lover of chastity, laying aside his habit, began to discipline himself severely with his cord, saying: "Brother Ass, thus dost thou deserve to be treated, thus to be beaten. Thou art unworthy to wear the religious habit, the sign of purity. Go thy way, then, whither thou wilt, for thus shalt thou go." And then in marvellous fervor of spirit he left his cell, and went out into the garden and plunged into a heap of snow which had just then fallen. Having done this, he gathered the snow in his hands and made seven heaps, which setting before him, he thus discoursed with his interior man: "Behold," said he, "this largest heap is thy wife; these four are thy two sons and thy two daughters; the other two are thy servant and thine handmaid; and for all these thou art bound to provide. Make haste, then, and provide clothing for them, lest they perish with cold. But if the solicitude for so many trouble thee, then be thou solicitous to serve one Lord alone." Then the tempter, being vanquished, departed, and the holy man returned victorious to his cell; and by the intensity of that external cold, to which he had subjected himself, the interior fire of temptation was so perfectly extinguished, that from that moment he never felt it in the slightest degree. Now a certain friar who was watching in prayer, beheld all these things by the clear light of the moon. And when the man of God knew what he had seen, he made known to him the temptation which he had endured, forbidding him, so long as he should live, to make known what he had seen to any living man.

And he not only taught the brethren thus to mortify the flesh, and to bridle its inclinations, but to keep a most careful watch over all the exterior senses, by which death finds an entrance to the soul. He bade them carefully to avoid all needless intercourse and familiarity with women, which is an occasion of ruin to many; affirming that the weak are ruined thereby, and the strongest in spirit made weak. And he was wont to say that, for any but a man of the most approved virtue, it was as easy (in words of the Holy Scripture) to walk in the midst of fire without being burnt, as thus to converse without receiving injury thereby. So faithfully did he turn away his eyes lest they should behold vanity, that, as he once said to one of his companions, he hardly knew any woman by sight. So dangerous did he account it to give admission to any images which might rekindle the quenched fire of temptation, or stain the purity of the soul. He affirmed that it was a frivolous thing to converse with women, except in the confessional, or to give them some short instruction, profitable to their salvation and suitable to religious modesty. "For what," said he, "has a religious to do with women, unless it be when they piously ask him to give them counsel how to do penance, or to follow a life of greater perfection? Where there is too great security, there is less watchfulness against the enemy; and if the devil can take hold of a man by a single hair, he will soon make it grow into a beam."

He taught them above all things to avoid idleness, as the sink of all evil thoughts, showing by his own example how to tame the lazy and rebellious flesh by continual disciplines and useful labors. Hence he called his body *Brother Ass,* saying that it was to be laden with heavy burthens, beaten with many stripes, and fed with poor and scanty food. If he saw anyone wandering about idle, and eating the fruit of other men's labor, he called him *Brother Fly,* because doing no good himself, he went about spoiling the good done by others, becoming thus vile and hateful to all. Therefore, he often said: "I would have my brethren to labor and strive, and not to give place by idleness to unlawful thoughts or idle words."

According to the Gospel precept, he would have the brethren to observe silence—that is, to carefully abstain at all times from evil words, seeing that they must give account thereof at the day of judgment; and if he found some brother to be given to foolish talking, he severely reproved him, affirming that modest taciturnity is no slight virtue, but the guardian of purity of heart; and that *life and death* are said to be *in the power of the tongue,* not so much with reference to the taste as to the speech. But although he sought with all his power to lead the brethren to austerity of life, he was not pleased with an indiscreet austerity, devoid of the bowels of compassion, and of the salt of discretion. For when, on a certain night, one of the brethren, from excessive abstinence was so pinched with hunger that he could find no rest, the good shepherd, hearing of the imminent peril of his sheep, brought bread; and lest he should be ashamed to eat it, he began first to eat before him, thus sweetly inviting him to eat. And the brother, overcoming his shame, took the bread, rejoicing that, by the wise consideration of his pastor, he was delivered from that bodily danger, and receiving at the same time no small edification from the holy man's example. The next morning the man of God called the brethren together, and made known to them what had happened in the night, adding the following admonition: "Take example, my brethren, not from the food eaten, but from the charity which caused it to be eaten." And he exhorted them to follow discretion, which is the charioteer of all the virtues; not that discretion which is taught by the prudence of the flesh, but that which Christ has taught us in His most sacred life, which is the example of all perfection. And because it is impossible for a man still encompassed with the infirmities of the flesh so perfectly to follow that spotless and crucified Lamb as never to contract any pollution by the way, therefore he strongly enforced upon them this truth, that whosoever would attain to a life of perfection must cleanse his conscience daily with abundance of tears. And although he had attained a marvellous purity of mind and body, he ceased not—regardless of the danger to his bodily health—to purify his mental sight by continual tears. Now, by this continual weeping he brought on a grievous malady in his eyes, and the physicians would have persuaded him to restrain his tears; but the holy man replied, "It is not fitting, Brother Physician, that for the love of that light which we have here below, in common with the flies, we should shut out the least ray of the eternal light which visits us from above; for the soul has not received the light for the sake of the body, but the body for the sake of the soul. I would, therefore, choose rather to lose the light of the body than to repress those tears by which the interior eyes are purified, that so they may see God, lest I should thus quench the spirit of devotion." Having been often counselled by the physicians, and also earnestly besought by the brethren to suffer the application of a cautery for the relief of his eyes, the man of God humbly assented, seeing that the remedy would be at once salutary and painful. The surgeon was therefore sent for, who placed the iron instrument in the fire. The servant consoled his shuddering body, as if it had been a friend, saying to the fire: "Oh, brother fire, the Most High has created thee glorious, mighty, beautiful, and useful above all other creatures. Be thou propitious and healthful to me at this hour. I beseech the great Lord, Who created thee, so sweetly to temper thy heat that I may be able to endure it." When he had finished his prayer he made the Sign of the Cross upon the red iron, and firmly waited its application. Then was the seething iron driven deep into the tender flesh, making a deep gash from the ear to the eyebrow. When he was asked concerning the pain caused by the fire, the holy man made answer: "Praise the Most High, my brethren, for I tell you truly that I have neither felt heat nor suffered from the burning iron;" and, turning to the surgeon, he said: "If the flesh is not sufficiently burnt, burn it again." And the surgeon, when he beheld the might of the spirit in the weakness of the flesh, marvelled greatly, and extolled that divine miracle, saying: "I tell you, brothers, I have seen wonders today." The man of God had attained to such a degree of purity that his flesh was subject to his spirit, and his spirit to God in a wonderful harmony and agreement, and all creatures were thus in marvellous subjection to his will and command, who was himself the faithful servant of the Creator.

Another time, when the servant of God was laboring under a grievous sickness, at the hermitage of St. Urban, feeling that nature was sinking, he asked for a cup of wine, and when they told him that there was no wine there to give him, he commanded them to bring him water, which he blessed with the Sign of the Cross. Then that which had been pure water was changed at once into excellent wine, and what the poverty of that desert place could not afford was obtained by the purity of the holy man. No sooner had he tasted it as wine than his strength was suddenly restored; so that the change of the water into wine, and the renovation of his lost strength thereby, bore twofold testimony that he had perfectly laid aside the old man, and clothed himself with the new.

And not only did creatures obey the will of the servant of God, but the Providence of the Creator condescended also to his good pleasure. For it happened once that, being weak and worn in body by many infirmities, which came upon him at one time, he desired to excite himself to spiritual joy and consolation by hearing some instrument of music, which the decorum of religion would not permit him to ask for at the hand of man, and lo! A great company of Angels surrounded him to fulfill his desire. As he was watching one night, and meditating upon the Lord, he suddenly heard the sound of a harp of wonderful harmony and most sweet melody. He saw no one, but the sound seemed to come nearer, and then was heard again afar off, showing that the players were passing backwards and forwards. His spirit, being all absorbed in God, was so filled with the sweetness of that harmony that he seemed to be already in another world. This was not hidden from some of the friars who were most familiar with him, who often perceived, by most certain indications and manifest signs, that he was visited by the Lord with such frequent and exceeding consolations as could not be concealed.

Another time, as the holy man was preaching between Lombardy and the March of Treviso, he was overtaken by night, with a friar as his companion, on the banks of the river Po; and the road being full of many and great dangers, as well from the darkness as from the river, and the waters which overflowed therefrom, his companion said to the holy man: "Father, pray that we may be delivered from the present danger." The man of God made answer with great confidence, "God is powerful if it shall please His most sweet mercy, He will dispel the darkness, and bestow upon us the blessing of light." He had hardly said these words, when, behold, by the divine power, so bright a light began to shine around them, that while to all others the night was dark as before, they not only saw the path before them, but a wide tract of country around! Led, therefore, by this light, by which they were corporally directed and spiritually comforted, they travelled on for a long distance unto the hospice whither they went, singing praises to God the while. Consider what was the purity and virtue of this man, at whose command fire tempered its fierceness, water changed its taste, Angels came to soothe him with their melody, and a light from Heaven shone forth for his guidance! Thus proving that the whole framework of the universe does homage and service to him who thus purifies and sanctifies his senses.

Chapter VI

HE man of God was filled to overflowing with humility, which is the glory and the guardian of all other virtues. In his own estimation he was a grievous sinner, though he was in truth the mirror and the glory of all sanctity. Upon this foundation he studied to build up himself; having laid, as a wise architect, that foundation which he had learnt from Christ. He was wont to say that the Son of God had descended from the bosom of His Father to our lowliness, that so by His example, as well as by His words, He, our Lord and Master, might teach us humility; and therefore, as the true disciple of Christ, he sought to abase himself, both in his own eyes and in the eyes of others, remembering the words of our Divine Master: "That which is highly esteemed among men is hateful in the sight of God." And he had these words continually in his mouth: "What a man is in the eyes of God, so much he is, and no more." He held it, therefore, to be a folly to be elated by the favors of the world, and thus he rejoiced in contempt, and was troubled at praise. He loved rather to meet with one who blamed him than with one who praised him, knowing that reproof leads to amendment, while praises excite to sin. And because the people often extolled his sanctity, he commanded certain of the brethren that, contrariwise, they should revile him, and address to him words of contempt; and when a brother (though against his will) called him a villain, an hireling, a useless person, with a joyful heart and countenance he made answer: "May the Lord bless thee, my dearest son, for thou speakest truly, and such words it befits the son of Peter Bernardone to hear." And that he might make himself contemptible to all, he was not ashamed when preaching to manifest his defects before all the people.

It happened once that, being grievously sick, he relaxed somewhat of the rigor of his abstinence for the recovery of his health. No sooner had he recovered his bodily strength than, filled with self-contempt, he determined to take shame to his body. "It is not fitting," he said, "that the people should account me a mortified man, while I secretly indulge my body." He rose, therefore, being inflamed with the spirit of holy humility, and having called together the people into the marketplace of Assisi, together with many friars whom he brought with him, he entered into the principal church, and having placed a cord round his neck, he commanded them to drag him, half-naked, to a stone on which condemned malefactors were wont to be placed. And mounting upon this stone, although he was suffering from ague and excessive weakness, and the weather was intensely cold, he preached with great force and energy to the people there assembled, affirming that he in nowise deserved to be honored by them as a spiritual man, but rather to be despised by all, as one carnal and gluttonous. All the assembly marvelled greatly at so strange a spectacle; and well knowing his austerity, they were pierced with compunction, and exclaimed that such humility was rather to be admired than within the reach of imitation. And although, indeed, such an act may rather be called a miracle than an example, nevertheless, it was a true lesson of perfect humility, by which everyone who would follow Christ is taught to despise the testimony of the world's transitory praise, and to repress the pride of vain boasting, and confute the falsehood of dissimulation.

Many such things he did, that he might appear outwardly a vile vessel of dishonor, possessing within the true spirit of sanctification. He studied to conceal the gifts of the Lord in the secret of his breast, lest, turning to his glory, they might become the occasion of his ruin. When he heard himself praised and blessed by many, he would often say: "I may yet have sons and daughters; you cannot safely praise me. No man is to be praised whose end is uncertain." This, to those who praised him; and to himself: "Francis, if a robber had received such graces as thou hast received, he would be far more grateful than thou." And he often said to the brethren: "No man ought wickedly to pride himself upon such things as a sinner can do. A sinner," he said, "can fast, pray, weep, mortify his flesh; this only he cannot do—be faithful to his Lord. In this, then, we may glory—if we give Him the glory which is due to Him, if we serve Him faithfully, if we ascribe all His gifts to Him." Now this evangelical merchant, that he might make the greater profit, and spend every moment of his life in laying up merit, ever chose to be a subject rather than a superior: to obey rather than to command. Therefore, laying aside his office of Minister-General, he desired to be under the Guardian, that he might in all things obey his will. For he declared that, so abundant is the fruit of holy obedience, that to those who place their neck beneath its yoke, no place and no time shall be without its profit. Therefore, he was accustomed to promise obedience to the friar who went with him as his companion; which promise he was most careful to fulfill. He said one day to the brethren: "Amongst many gifts which our Lord in His goodness has bestowed upon me, He has granted me this grace—to obey with the same readiness a novice who had been but an hour in religion, were he set over me as my superior, as the most ancient and discreet amongst the brethren."

"The subject," he was wont to say, "should look upon his prelate not as a man, but as the representative of Him for Whose love he is subject to him. For the more contemptible is he who commands, the more pleasing to God is the humility of him who obeys."

Being once asked who could be counted truly obedient, he brought forward the example of a dead body. "Take," he said, "an inanimate corpse, and place it where thou wilt. Thou wilt see that it will not resist thee in any wise. It will not murmur at the place thou givest it, nor cry out if thou leavest it there. If thou shalt place it on a throne, it will not look upwards, but always downwards. If thou clothe it in purple, it will but look the paler. "Thus," said he, "is it with the truly obedient man. If he be removed, he considers not wherefore; he cares not where he is placed, nor asks to be transferred to another office. If he be exalted, he preserves his accustomed humility; and accounts himself the more unworthy the greater honor he receives."

Another day, he said to his companion: "I shall never account myself a friar minor until I attain to the state which I shall now describe to thee. Suppose I am a prelate set over the brethren, and I go to the chapter to preach and admonish them, and at the end of my discourse they tell me that I am not fit to be over them; that I do not know how to speak; that I am illiterate, foolish, and simple. Suppose that I am then cast out with shame, amidst the derision of all. I tell thee that unless I endure these things with an even countenance, an even gladness of heart, and an even sanctity of purpose, I am no friar minor." And he added: "In the loss of dignity, in the absence of praise, in humble subjection, there is great profit to the soul. Why, therefore, when time has been given us to profit withal, do we seek rather for peril than for profit?"

From humility, therefore, Francis desired that his friars should be called *minors,* and that the prelates of his Order should bear the name of minister, both to fulfill the words of the Gospel, which they had promised to observe; and also that his disciples might learn by the very name they bear that they have come to the school of the humble Jesus to learn humility. For the Master of humility, Jesus Christ, that He might form His disciples to perfect humility, said: "Whosoever will be greatest among you let him be your minister, and whosoever will be the first among you he shall be your servant." Therefore, when the man of God was asked by the Cardinal of Ostia, the protector and chief promoter of the Order of Friars Minor, who was afterwards raised, according to the prediction of the holy man, to the supreme Pontificate under the name of Gregory the Ninth—when he was asked by this great man to consent to the promotion of his brethren to ecclesiastical dignities, he made answer thus: "My Lord, my friars have been called *minors* that they might not presume to become *majors.* If thou wilt have them to bear fruit in the Church of God, keep and preserve them in this their state and vocation, and never suffer them to rise to ecclesiastical prelatures."

And inasmuch as he preferred humility to honors, both in himself and in others, God, Who loves the humble, judged him worthy of the highest honor, as was shown by a heavenly vision vouchsafed to a very devout and holy friar. For this friar, being in company with the holy man, entered with him into a certain deserted church, and there, as he was praying fervently, he fell into an ecstasy, and amid many thrones in Heaven he saw one more glorious than all the rest, adorned with precious stones of most glorious brightness. And marvelling at the surpassing brightness of that throne, he began anxiously to consider within himself who should be found worthy to fill it. Then he heard a voice saying to him: "This was the throne of one of the fallen angels, and now it is reserved for the humble Francis." When the friar had recovered from his ecstasy, he went forth from the church, following the blessed man, as was his wont. And as they went on their way conversing, according to their custom, of God, the friar (remembering his vision) bethought him to ask the man of God what he thought of himself. To which Christ's humble servant made reply: "I think myself to be the greatest of sinners." And when the brother answered that he could not with a safe conscience say or think such a thing, he added: "If Christ had shown to the most wicked man on earth such mercy as He has shown to me, I believe assuredly that that man would have been far more grateful to God than I have been." By this wonderful humility the brother was confirmed in the truth of the vision which he had seen, knowing by the testimony of the holy Gospel that the humble shall be exalted to that excellent glory from which the proud shall be cast down.

Another time, when Francis was praying in a certain deserted church, in the province of Massa, near Mount Casale, he was enlightened in spirit to know that some sacred relics were there concealed. Grieving that they had been so long defrauded of their due honor, he commanded his brethren to remove them; but being compelled by some urgent cause to leave the place, the sons forgot their Father's command, and lost the merit of obedience. One day when the holy Mass was about to be celebrated, on removing the first covering of the altar, they found some beautiful and fragrant bones, which they recognized to be the relics of the saints, brought thither not by the hand of man but by the power of God. The man of God, returning soon afterwards, inquired whether they had fulfilled his command concerning the relics. The brethren humbly confessed their neglect of obedience, and obtained pardon, together with penance, for their fault. Then said the holy man: "Blessed be the Lord my God, Who Himself hath done that which you ought to have done." Consider diligently the care which Divine Providence takes of our ashes, and behold how excellent in the eyes of God was the virtue of the humble Francis. For when man cared not to fulfill his command, God was obedient to his desire.

Coming on a certain day to Imola, he humbly besought the Bishop of that city to give him permission to call the people together to hear him preach. But the Bishop answered roughly: "It is sufficient, friar, that I preach to my people myself." And the humble Francis bowed his head and went his way. But after the short space of an hour he came back again. When the Bishop, with some displeasure, inquired what he came again to ask, he made answer, in all humility of heart and speech: "My Lord, if a father sends his son out at one door, there is nothing left for him but to return by another." Then the Bishop, being vanquished by this humility, embraced him with a joyful countenance, saying, "Thou and all thy brethren shall have a general license to preach throughout my diocese, as the reward of thy holy humility."

It came to pass that he went to Arezzo at a time when that city, being torn by intestine wars and seditions, was even nigh to its ruin. As he lodged in a suburb outside the walls, he saw a multitude of demons rejoicing over the city, and instigating the angry citizens to destroy each other. In order to disperse these seditious powers of the air, he sent as his herald Brother Sylvester, a man simple as a dove, saying to him: "Go

to the gates of the city, and there, in the Name of
Almighty God, command the demons by virtue of holy
obedience, that without delay they depart from that
place." The obedient friar, having heard these words,
set forth to fulfill the command; and singing the praises
of the Lord as he went, he soon stood before the city
gates, and cried with a loud voice: "In the Name of
Almighty God, and by the command of His servant
Francis, I bid you all, infernal demons, to depart far
from hence." No sooner had he spoken than the tumult
in the city was appeased, and all the citizens, in great
tranquillity, began to revise the statutes and regula-
tions of the city, that so they might be duly observed.
Thus the fierce pride of the demons, which had enslaved
the miserable city, was overcome by the wisdom of the
poor, and the humility of Francis restored it to peace
and safety. For the great virtue of humble obedience
obtained the mastery over those mutinous and rebellious spirits, bringing down and humbling their fierce
pride, and putting their evil will utterly to flight. The
demons of pride ever fly from the sublime virtue of
humility; unless, for its more careful custody and preser-
vation, the divine clemency permits them to tempt and
trouble the humble, as the Apostle Paul writes of himself, and as Francis proved by his own experience.

Cardinal Leo, of Sante Croce, having once prayed
him to remain with him awhile at Rome, Francis humbly
consented to his desire, for the reverence and love
which he bore so great a man. On the first night, as
he desired to take some rest after his prayers, the
demons arose in great fury against the Soldier of Christ,
and having severely beaten him, they left him as it
were half dead. When they were gone, Francis called
his companion, who came to him at once, and to him
the holy man related what had happened, adding: "I
believe, brother, that the demons, who can do nothing

but by the disposition of Divine Providence, have beaten me now so cruelly, because it is not well that I should abide in the courts of princes. My brethren, who dwell in poor places, will perhaps think when they see me living with Cardinals, that I am meddling in worldly matters, or seeking after honors, or enjoying delicacies. Therefore I judge it far better that he who is to give an example to others should fly from courts, and dwell humbly among the humble in humble places, that he may be able to strengthen those who suffer poverty and are ill at ease, seeing that he endures the same things himself." The next morning, therefore, he offered his humble excuses to the Cardinal, and took his leave with the brethren.

And as the holy man greatly abhorred pride, which is the origin of all evils, and disobedience, her most evil daughter, he never failed to accept and commend the humility of penitents. It happened once that a certain friar was brought before him, who had committed some little fault against the rule of obedience, that he might be corrected by the discipline of his justice. The holy man perceiving, by evident signs, that this brother was really and deeply contrite, was moved by his love of humility to pardon him. Nevertheless, that the facility of the pardon might not give occasion to others to sin, he commanded that the friar's cowl should be taken from him and cast into the fire, that all might learn how great and signal a punishment is due to disobedience. When the cowl had remained for some time in the midst of the fire, he commanded it to be drawn forth from the flames, and restored to the brother, now humbly penitent. Marvellous to relate, when the cowl was taken out of the midst of the flames, it bore upon it no vestige of fire. And thus, by one and the same miracle, God commended the virtue of the holy man and the humility of the patient. Worthy, therefore, of all men to be followed is the humility of Francis, which even in his earthly life raised him to such dignity, inclined God to his desires, changed the affections of men, bowed the proud demons to his will, and bridled the voracity of fire at the mere sign of his pleasure. Humility it is which exalts its possessors, and while it shows reverence to all men, is honored by all men in return.

Chapter VII

OF HIS LOVE OF POVERTY, AND THE WONDERFUL
PROVISION MADE FOR ALL HIS WANTS BY GOD.

MIDST the other graces which Francis received from the bountiful giver of all good gifts, he merited by a special prerogative to increase continually in the treasure of simplicity by the love of most deep poverty. For the holy man considering this poverty to have been ever the familiar and beloved companion of the Son of God, and seeing that it was now cast out by all the world, so bound himself to it in perpetual espousals, that he forsook for it not only his father and mother, but also distributed all things whatsoever which he had in his power to give. No man was ever so covetous of gold as he of poverty, nor did any man ever so carefully guard a treasure as he this pearl of the Gospel. Nothing gave him so much offence as to see anything in the brethren not wholly in accordance with poverty. Certain it is, that from his entrance into religion, even unto his death, he contented himself with a single tunic and cord. He frequently called to mind, with many tears, the poverty of Jesus Christ and His Mother; and affirmed *that* to be the queen of virtues, which shone so gloriously in the King of kings, and in the Queen His Mother. Therefore when his brethren once asked him in conclave, by which virtue we become dearest to Christ, he, as if opening to them the secret of his heart, replied: "Know, my brethren, that poverty is the special way to salvation; for it is the food of humility, and the root of perfection, whose fruits, although hidden, are manifold. This is the treasure of which we read in Gospel, which was hidden in the field; to buy which a man should sell all that he hath, and in comparison with which all that can be given for its purchase is to be accounted as nothing. And he who would attain to this height of perfection must lay aside not only worldly prudence, but even all knowledge of letters, that thus stripped of all things he may come to see what is the power of the Lord, and cast himself naked into the arms of the Crucified. Neither does he perfectly renounce the world who keeps a place for the indulgence of his own senses in the secret of his heart." And many times when he spoke to his brethren of poverty he would quote these words of the Gospel: "The foxes have holes, and the birds of the air nests; but the Son of Man hath not where to lay His Head." Therefore, he taught the brethren that, after the manner of the poor, they should build for themselves poor little huts, and that they should not look upon even these as their own, but dwell in them as pilgrims in the houses of others. For he said that it was the manner of pilgrims to dwell under the roof of other men, longing for the day when they should peacefully return to their own country. He would sometimes command that houses already built should be pulled down, or that the friars should remove from them, if he saw anything therein which savored of proprietorship, or that seemed too sumptuous to befit evangelical poverty; for this he said was the foundation of the Order, which, if it were first laid, the whole religious structure would rest upon it, being strengthened by its strength; whereas, if the foundation fail, the whole edifice comes to ruin.

He taught also, as he had learned by revelation, that the beginning of holy religion must be the fulfillment of these words of the Gospel: "Go and sell all that thou

hast, and give to the poor." Therefore, he would admit
none to the Order except such as would strip themselves of all things, retaining nothing for themselves,
as well in obedience to the words of the Holy Gospel,
as to avoid the danger and scandal which the reser-
vation of worldly goods would occasion to the soul.
Therefore, when a certain man, in the March of Ancona,
asked to be received into the Order, the true Patriarch
of the poor replied: "If thou wilt become one of the
poor of Christ, distribute thy goods to the poor." The
man went his way, and being led astray by carnal affection, he left his property to his kindred, and not to the
poor. When the holy man heard thereof he severely
rebuked him, saying: "Go thy way, Brother Fly, for thou
hast in no wise gone forth from thy kindred and from
thy father's house. Thou hast given thy goods to thy
family, and hast defrauded the poor; thou art not worthy to be a follower of holy poverty. Thou hast begun
with the flesh, and hast sought to raise a spiritual
building upon a ruinous foundation." Then this carnal
man returned home, and reclaiming his goods, which
he would not give up to the poor, he quickly forsook
his holy purpose.

Another time there was such poverty at St. Mary of
the Portiuncula, that there was not wherewithal to
supply the necessary wants of the brethren who came
thither. Wherefore the Vicar of the man of God came
to him, beseeching him that on account of the poverty
of the brethren he would give permission to all the
novices on their entrance to keep somewhat of their
property, that so the brethren might have something
to fall back upon in time of need. To whom the holy
man replied, being enlightened with knowledge from
on high: "God forbid, beloved brother, that for any man
whomsoever we should thus sin against the rule. I
would rather have thee strip the altar of the glorious

Virgin, should necessity so require, than infringe in the slightest degree the vow of poverty, and the due observance of the Gospel precept. For rather would the Blessed Virgin see her altar unadorned, and the counsel of the Holy Gospel perfectly observed, than that her altar should be ornamented, and the counsel of her Son set at nought."

Another day, as the man of God was passing with his companion by the city of Bari, in Apulia, he found a heavy purse on the way, which was all swollen as if full of money. His companion showed the purse to the poor man of Christ, and earnestly besought him to let him take it from the ground, and distribute the money among the poor. The man of God refused, affirming that there was some diabolical delusion connected with that purse, and that the brother would persuade him to do a sinful action and not a good work, by taking the property of another to give away. So they left that place, and hastened forward on their way. But the friar could not be appeased, being deluded by a vain show of pity, and continued to urge the holy man, as if he cared not to relieve the misery of the poor. Then Francis, in his meekness, agreed to return to the place, not to fulfill the will of the brother, but to detect the fraud of the devil. Having returned to the place with the friar and a certain young man who was travelling that way, and having first prayed to God, he commanded his companion to take up the purse. The brother did so trembling, being struck with sudden terror at the diabolical presence; but in obedience to the holy man's command he overcame his fear, and stretched out his hand to the purse. When, behold, a great serpent issued therefrom, and immediately vanishing, together with it, revealed the diabolical deception to the brother. The delusion of the cunning adversary being thus made known, the holy man said to his companion: "Money, my brother, is to the servants of God nothing else but the devil and a venomous serpent."

Soon afterwards a marvellous thing befell the holy man, who had gone for some urgent cause to the city of Siena. On the plain which is between Campiglia and Santo Quirico he met three women, in appearance poor, and in stature, age, and countenance exactly resembling one another. They saluted him after this singular manner: "Welcome!" they said, "to the Lady Poverty." And when the true lover of poverty heard this he was filled with unspeakable joy, seeing that there was no salutation so dear to him as this which he had now heard. The women suddenly disappeared, and the brethren in his company observing the marvellous similarity between them, the manner of their salutation, and the strange suddenness of their disappearance, considered (not without reason) that some great mystery was hereby signified concerning the holy man. It would seem, indeed, that by these women, so poor, and so like one another, who met him and saluted him after so singular a fashion, and so suddenly disappeared, was signified the beauty of evangelical perfection, which consists in chastity, poverty, and obedience, all which shone forth in the holy man in equal beauty and glory, although he glorified in the privilege of poverty rather than in any other thing, being wont to call it, now his *mother*, now his *spouse*, now his *lady*. In this he desired to surpass all others, because by this he had learnt to account himself inferior to all others. And if he sometimes met with someone who in exterior habit seemed poorer than himself, he would immediately reprove himself, and excite himself to do the like, as if in the continual battle which he waged for his lady, Poverty, he feared to be overcome. One day he met a poor man on the road, and looking upon his misery he was pierced to the heart, and said in a lamentable voice to his companion: "The poverty of this man makes me greatly ashamed, because, whereas we have chosen poverty in exchange for great riches, he shines forth therein far more brightly than we."

For the love of holy poverty, this servant of Almighty God loved far better to live upon the alms which he begged from door to door than upon that which was freely offered to him. And when he was sometimes invited by some great person to dine with him, knowing that he should, as a mark of honor, be made to sit down at an abundant table, he went first to ask for broken pieces of bread at the neighboring houses, and thus, in the wealth of poverty, he sat down to eat. Now it happened one day that he was invited by the Cardinal of Ostia, who had an exceeding affection for this poor man of Christ, and when the bishop complained that it was against his honor, when he was bidden to eat at his table, that he should go about asking for alms, the servant of God replied: "My lord, by thus acting I have greatly honored thee, inasmuch as I have honored a Lord greater than thou. For the Lord delighteth in poverty, and more than all in that beggary which is embraced for Christ. Nor will I lay aside that regal dignity which our Lord Jesus Christ assumed when he became poor that He might enrich us by His poverty, and so make the poor in spirit to be kings and heirs of the kingdom of Heaven. I will not lay it aside, I say, for the gift of all the false riches which, for a short space, are granted to thee." He would oftentimes exhort the brethren to ask for alms in words such as these—"Go," said he, "for the Friars Minor have been given in these last days to the world, that the elect, by their means, may obtain the praise of the Great Judge, and hear these most sweet words: 'Inasmuch as you have done it unto one of the least of these My brethren, you have done it unto Me:'" And he said that it was a joyful thing to beg under the name of a Friar Minor, seeing that it is the very name used by the mouth of the Master of evangelical truth when He spoke of the reward of the just. It was his practice, when opportunity offered, to go begging on the principal Feasts, saying that in holy poverty the prophet's words are fulfilled: "Man shall eat the Bread of Angels; for that assuredly," said he, "is the Bread of Angels which is asked for the love of God, and, by the suggestion of Angels, is given by the charity of those at whose doors it is begged by holy poverty." Therefore, when he once passed the holy day of Easter in a distant hermitage, so far from the dwellings of men that it was not possible to go forth to beg, in memory of Him Who appeared on that day in the form of a pilgrim to the disciples going to Emmaus, he asked alms of his own brethren as a poor pilgrim; which, when he had humbly received, he admonished them in many holy words that, passing through the desert of this world as pilgrims, and strangers, and true Hebrews, they should celebrate, in continual poverty of spirit, the true Pasch of the Lord, that is, the passage from this world to the Father. And, since in asking alms he was moved not by covetousness but by liberty of spirit, God, the Father of the poor, ever extended a special care over him.

It happened once that the servant of God was grievously sick in the city of Norsia, and being brought back to Assisi by messengers sent from the city, on account of the great devotion that was borne him there, they who carried the holy man came to a poor little town named Sarziano; and it being the hour of dinner, and all being hungry, they went to buy some food, and, finding nothing, they returned empty-handed. "Then," said the holy man, "you have found nothing, because you trust more in your *flies* than in the Lord,"—for by flies he was wont to signify money; "return, therefore," said he, "to the houses you have already visited, and humbly ask for alms, offering the love of God in return. Nor do you account this in your false judgment to be a vile thing, for, after sin committed, God, the great almsgiver, grants to all, both worthy and unworthy, all things needful as an alms." Then, laying aside their false shame, they went and asked for alms, and more was freely given to them for the love of God than by the money they had been able to procure. For the hearts of the poor men who dwelt in that place being pierced by the divine inspiration, they offered not their possessions only, but themselves; and thus it befell, that the necessity which by money could not be relieved, the rich and abundant poverty of Francis supplied.

At the time when he lay sick at the hermitage near Rieti, a certain physician was accustomed frequently to visit and attend him. And as Christ's poor man was unable to make him a due return for his labors, the most bountiful God—lest he should lack a present remuneration—rewarded his pious service (in the place of his poor patient) by this extraordinary favor. The house of this physician, which he had built anew with the fruit of his labors, was threatened with approaching ruin by a fissure in the wall, which reached from the top to the bottom of the house, so that it seemed impossible for human art or industry to prevent its fall. But he, trusting wholly in the merits of the holy man, asked his companion, with great faith and devotion, to give him something which the hands of the man of God had touched. Therefore, having with much importunity and many prayers obtained a small piece of his hair, he placed it in the fissure; and the next morning he found the aperture so solidly closed, that it was impossible either to extract the hair or to perceive the slightest vestige of the crack. And so it was, that he who sedulously ministered to the bodily infirmities of the servant of God was preserved from his own peril and the ruin of his house.

Another time, when the man of God wished to go to a certain desert place, that he might give himself the more freely to contemplation, being very weak, he rode upon an ass belonging to a poor man. It being a hot summer's day, the poor man, as he followed the servant of Christ, became weary with the long way and the steep ascent, and beginning to faint with fatigue and burning thirst, he called after the Saint: "Behold," he said, "I shall die of thirst unless I can find a little water at once to refresh me." Then without delay the man of God got off the ass, and kneeling down with his hands stretched out to Heaven, he ceased not to pray till he knew that he was heard. Having finished his prayer he said to the man: "Hasten to yonder rock, and there shalt thou find living water, which Christ the merciful hath even now brought forth therefrom that thou mayest drink." Oh! marvellous goodness of God, Who thus easily inclines to the prayer of His servants! The thirsty man drank of the water drawn from the hard rock by the power of prayer. Never was flowing water in that place before; neither, however diligently sought for, could it ever be found there afterwards.

How, by the merits of His poor servant, Christ multiplied food on the sea, shall be noted hereafter in its place; suffice it here to say that, by a small alms which had been given to him, he preserved many mariners from famine and the danger of death for many days together.

Whence it may be seen, that this servant of Almighty God was made like unto Moses in bringing water out of the rock, and to Eliseus in the multiplication of food. Therefore, let the poor man of Christ lay aside all distrust. For if the poverty of Francis was so abundantly sufficient to supply by its wonderful power the wants of all those who in any way assisted him, so that they wanted neither food nor drink, nor house, when all supply of money and all natural power and faculties failed them, much more shall they deserve to receive those things which the order of Divine Providence is accustomed to grant indifferently to all men. If, I say, the dry rock at the voice of the poor gave forth abundant water for the need of that poor thirsty man, never will our Lord deny anything to those who have left all things for the Author of all things.

Chapter VIII

OF HIS TENDER PIETY, AND HOW EVEN CREATURES
DEVOID OF REASON WERE OBEDIENT TO HIS WILL.

RUE piety, which, according to the Apostle, is profitable for all things, had so filled and penetrated the heart of Francis, the servant of God, that he was seen to be wholly subject to its dominion. He was thereby raised to God by devotion, transformed into Christ by compassion, brought near by condescension to his neighbor; and by the love which he bore all creatures he attracted them to himself, even as Adam in his state of innocency.

And as he was thus tenderly affectionate to all, so especially when he saw souls redeemed by the precious Blood of Christ Jesus to be defiled by any stain of sin, he mourned over them with such tenderness of commiseration, as if like a mother he were daily bringing them forth to Christ. And this was the principal cause of his veneration for all the ministers of the Word of God, as for those who raise up seed for Christ, their deceased Brother, crucified for sinners, and with pious solicitude rear and govern the children whom they bring forth to Him. And this office of mercy he affirmed to be the more acceptable to the Father of Mercies if fulfilled with perfect charity; and therefore he labored after this in his own person, rather by example than by words, rather by the language of tears than by the eloquence of speech. For he said that that preacher is worthy to be bewailed with many tears who is devoid of true piety, or who in his preaching seeks not the salvation of souls, but his own praise, or who destroys by the depravity of his life what he builds up by the truth of his doctrine. And he said that the brother is to be preferred, who, being simple and slow of speech, excites others to good by the force of his good example, and he gave this explanation of the verse: "The barren hath borne many children." "The barren," he said, "is a poor little friar, who has no office to bring forth children in the Church; but he shall bring forth many in the last judgment, for they who are now converted to Christ by his secret prayers shall then be ascribed by the Judge to his glory." "'He who hath borne many children hath become weak;' that is, the vain and loquacious preacher who rejoices now in many children, begotten (as he believes) by his own virtue, shall then acknowledge that he has no part in them."

Francis, therefore, desiring with his whole heart the salvation of souls, and being full of most fervent zeal for their conversion, was wont to say that he was perfumed with sweet odors, and, as it were, anointed with precious ointment, when he heard that, by the sweet odor of his brethren's sanctity diffused throughout the world, many were brought into the way of truth. And when he heard such tidings he rejoiced in spirit, and poured forth most abundant blessings upon those brethren who, by word or deed, brought sinners to the love of Christ. But they who by their evil deeds dishonor holy religion, incurred the most heavy sentence of his malediction. "By Thee," said he, "Most Holy Lord, by the whole heavenly court, and by me, Thy little one, let them be accursed, who by their evil example confound and destroy that which, by the holy brethren of this Order, Thou hast built up, and ceasest not still to build." And he was oftentimes so oppressed with sadness at the scandal thus given to the little ones of

Christ, that it seemed he would have even sunk under it, had he not been supported by the consolation of the divine mercy. As he was one day greatly troubled on this account, and was praying with an anxious heart to the Father of mercies for his children, he received this answer from the Lord: "Why art thou troubled, poor little one, as if I had in such wise set thee as a pastor over Mine Order, that thou shouldst forget that I am its chief Master? I have chosen thee, a simple man, for this office, that whatsoever I shall work in thee may be ascribed not to thee, but to divine grace. I have called, I will preserve, I will feed these my sheep; and if some be cut off, I will bring others into their place; and if they be not yet born, I will bring them into being; and by whatever attacks this poor religion shall be assailed, by My help it shall be preserved, and shall abide forever."

Francis abhorred detraction, as a vice most hostile to the fountain of grace and piety; he compared it to the bite of a most venomous and horrible serpent, accounting it to be most hateful to our good and gracious God, and affirming that detraction feeds upon the blood of souls, which it slays with the sword of the tongue. Hearing a friar once lessening the good fame of another, he turned to his Vicar, and said: "Arise, search diligently, and if thou shouldst find the accused brother innocent, let the accuser be severely corrected in the sight of all." He was wont to say that he who deprived his brother of his good fame should be deprived of his habit, nor should he venture to raise his eyes to the Lord until to the best of his power he had restored that which he had taken from him. "Detraction," he said, "is so much greater a sin than theft, as the law of Christ, which is fulfilled by charity, bids us seek after the health of the soul rather than of the body." Yet with exceeding tenderness of compassion did he minister to all bodily sufferings, whether penury, or want of any kind, sweetly commending the sufferer to Christ. Mercy, indeed, was born with him, but it received a two-fold increase by the infused charity of Christ, for truly his soul melted within him at the sight of poverty and sickness; and the comfort which his hand was unable to bestow, he gave by the affection of his heart.

It happened once that a certain poor man begged of him importunately, and was answered roughly by one of the brothers. When the pious lover of the poor heard it, he commanded the friar to lay aside his habit, and cast himself at the poor man's feet, acknowledging his fault, and begging him to pardon and pray for him. When he had humbly obeyed, our sweet Father said to him: "My brother, when thou seest a poor man, behold in him a mirror of the Lord, and of His poor Mother. In the sick, in like manner, consider that He bore our sicknesses."

Thus in all the poor this model of Christian poverty beheld the image of Christ, and so when he had received as an alms things necessary for the body, he not only liberally bestowed them upon any poor man whom he met on the way, but accounted that he was thus restoring to him what was rightfully his own. It happened once that he met a poor man, as he was returning from Siena wearing, by reason of sickness, a cloak over his habit. Beholding with a pitiful eye the misery of this poor man, "It is fitting," said he to his companion, "that we should restore this cloak to this poor man, for it is his, and I accepted it only until I should find someone poorer than myself." But his companion, considering the necessity of the compassionate Father, pertinaciously objected to his relieving others and neglecting himself. But he answered: "I should be accounted a thief by the great Almsgiver were I to withhold that which I wear

from him who has greater need of it than I." Therefore, he was accustomed to ask permission of those who
relieved his corporal necessities, to give away that which
he received from them to any he should meet with in
any greater need than himself. He spared nothing, neither cloak, nor tunic, nor books, nor even the ornaments of the altar, but would give all these things to
the poor to fulfill the office of mercy. Oftentimes when
he met a poor man on the way, laden with a heavy burden, he would take it on his own weak shoulders and
carry it for him.

The consideration of the common origin of all creatures filled him with overflowing tenderness for all;
and he called them all his brothers and sisters, because
they had all one origin with himself. But he bore the
sweetest and strongest affection to those whose natural qualities set forth the sweet meekness of Christ,
and by which He is therefore signified in Holy Scripture. He would frequently redeem lambs which were
being led to the slaughter, in memory of that most
meek Lamb Who, to redeem sinners, vouchsafed to be
led forth to die. It happened once, when the servant
of God abode at the Monastery of St. Verecundo, in the
diocese of Gubbio, that a sheep brought forth her lamb
in the night. A ferocious sow, which was in the place,
destroyed that innocent life with her ravenous jaws.
When the loving Father heard of it, he was moved with
compassion, and in memory of the Lamb without spot,
he began to lament over the death of the little creature before them all, saying: "Woe is me, brother lamb,
innocent animal representing Christ to men; accursed
be that evil beast which slew thee; let neither man
nor beast eat of its flesh forever." Marvellous to say,
the cruel sow at once fell sick, and after three days
paid the penalty of her evil deed by her own death.
Being cast into the convent ditch, her body long

remained there, dried up like a piece of wood. See, then, what chastisement shall befall the wickedness of men, if the ferocity of a beast was punished by so evil a death. Consider how marvellous was the piety, and how overflowing the sweetness of the servant of God, which caused even brute natures to pay him all the homage in their power. As he was passing through the plains round the city of Siena, he met with a large flock of sheep, which, when he saluted them benignly (as was his custom), all left their pasture, and ran to him, raising their heads and fixing their eyes upon him. And so gladsomely did they frolic round him that the friars and shepherds marvelled, beholding not only the lambs, but even the rams, exulting in his presence.

At another time, at St. Mary of the Portiuncula, a sheep was brought to the man of God which, because of the innocency and loving simplicity betokened by these creatures, he gladly received. The holy man taught the sheep that it should always praise God, and give no offence to the brethren; and the sheep, as if it had a sense of the piety of the man of God, carefully observed all his commandments. For when it heard the brethren singing in the choir, it would go into the church, and, unbidden, bend its knees, bleating, before the altar of the Virgin Mother of the Lamb. And when the most sacred Body of Christ was elevated in the holy Mass it would bend its knees; thus, by the reverence of a dumb animal, rebuking the irreverence of the undevout, and exciting the devout to greater veneration for the Sacrament of Christ.

Another time he kept a little lamb with him in the city of Rome, in reverence of the most meek Lamb of God, which he committed to the care of a noble lady, Jacoba di Settesoli. And the lamb, as if it had been trained in spiritual things by the holy man, would go with the lady to church, remain there with all reverence, and return with her as her inseparable companion. If the lady was late in rising in the morning, the lamb would come and push her with its little horns, and excite her by its bleatings, signs, and gestures to hasten to the church. Therefore, this lamb, the disciple of Francis, and so great a master of devotion, was kept by the lady as a marvellous and precious thing.

Another time, when the man of God was at Grecio, a live hare was brought to him, which, although it was placed upon the ground, that it might escape if it would, at the call of the loving Father leaped of its own accord into his bosom. And he, pressing it to him with tender affection, admonished it with motherly compassion not to let itself be taken again, and then set it free. But although it was many times placed upon the ground, that it might depart, it still returned into the Father's bosom, as if it had some hidden sense of the pitifulness of his heart; at last, by his command, it was carried safely by the brethren to a solitary place.

In like manner, a rabbit which was caught in an island on the Lake of Perugia, and brought to the man of God, while it fled from all others, committed itself fearlessly to his hands, and nestled in his bosom.

As he was passing by the Lake of Rieti, near the hermitage of Grecio, a fisherman, out of devotion, brought to him a water-fowl, which, having willingly accepted, he opened his hands to let it fly away, but it would not depart; then raising his eyes to heaven, he remained for a long time in prayer, and coming to himself (as it were), after the space of more than an hour, he sweetly reiterated his command that, giving praise to the Lord, it should depart. Then, receiving his holy benediction, it flew joyfully away.

In the same lake was found a great fish, which was brought to him alive. After his custom, he called it by the name of *brother,* and put it back again into the water, near the boat in which he was. But the fish gambolled in the water before the man of God, and, as if attracted by the love of him, would by no means depart from the boat, until he sent it away with his blessing.

Another day, as he was walking with a certain friar near the Lagunes of Venice, he saw a great multitude of birds sitting upon the branches of a tree, and singing aloud. Then he said to his companion, "Our sisters, the birds, praise their Creator; let us therefore go into the midst of them, and sing the Canonical Hours to the Lord." And when they went into the midst of them, the birds departed not from their place. But because, for the noise they made, the friars could not hear each other as they said the Hours, the holy man said to the birds: "My sisters, the birds, cease your singing until we have fulfilled our duty in praising God." And the birds hushed their singing at once, and remained silent until the Office was fully said, and they received permission from the man of God to resume their song. No sooner had he given them leave, than they began to sing after their wonted manner, on a fig-tree, near the cell of the man of God.

At St. Mary of the Angels, a grasshopper was continually chirping, which, by its song, excited the servant of God to praise the Lord; for he had learnt, even in the most insignificant creatures, to admire the wonderful works of the Creator. One day he called the grasshopper to him, which, as if it had been divinely admonished to obey, perched at once upon his hand. And he said to it, "Sing, my sister grasshopper; rejoice and praise the Lord thy Creator." And the creature began at once to chirp, and ceased not until, at the command of the Father, it sprang back again to its own place. Thus for eight days together it remained on that same branch, daily coming to the holy man at his command, and departing again when he sent it away. At length the man of God said to his companions: "Let us give leave to our sister grasshopper to depart, for she hath now sufficiently cheered us by her song, and for these eight days past hath excited us to praise our God." And immediately it departed, nor did it ever appear there again, as if it dared not in any wise transgress his command.

When he was sick at Siena, a certain nobleman sent him a live pheasant which had been just caught. No sooner did it see and hear the holy man, than so lovingly did it cleave to him, that it could not bear to be separated from him. For although it was often taken out of the cloister by the brethren into a vineyard hard by, that it might go whithersoever it would, it always flew back to the Father, as if it had been fed by him all the days of its life. Being afterwards given to a certain man, who, out of devotion, came often to visit the holy man, as if sorrowful at being taken away from that pitiful Father, the bird refused to eat. It was brought back again to the servant of God, and as soon as it saw him it gave signs of great joy, and began to eat with avidity.

When he came to the hermitage at Alvernia, to keep Lent in honor of the Archangel Michael, many different kinds of birds came flying round his cell with sweet songs and glad gestures, as if they rejoiced at his coming, and would invite that pious Father to remain amongst them. And when he saw it, he said to his companion: "I perceive, brother, that it is the Will of God that we should abide here awhile, seeing that our sisters, the birds, thus rejoice at our presence."

Now, while he abode there, a falcon, which had her nest in that place, made a loving friendship with him. For, by her cry, she gave notice to the holy man every night of the hour at which he was wont to rise to say the Divine Office. The great care which this bird took to wake him was most pleasing to the man of God, because it freed him from all danger of sloth and negligence. But when the servant of Christ was sick, and weaker than was his wont, the falcon spared his infirmity, and called him later than usual; for, as if she had been admonished by God, she awoke him with a gentle call at the break of day. And, assuredly, there seemed to be a divine presage, both in the exultation of the manifold kind of birds and in the cry of this falcon, of the sublime dignity to which the devoted servant and worshipper of God was soon to be raised on the wings of contemplation by the apparition of the Seraph.

While the holy man dwelt, at another time, at the hermitage of Grecio, the inhabitants of that place were troubled with many and divers evils, for a great multitude of ravenous wolves devoured not only beasts, but men, and the hail also yearly destroyed their corn and vines. When, therefore, the herald of the Holy Gospel was preaching to these afflicted men, he said to them, "I bid you believe, to the honor and glory of Almighty God, that all these plagues shall depart from you, and the Lord will look upon you, and will multiply your temporal goods, if you will believe my words and have mercy upon yourselves, and (having made a good confession) bring forth worthy fruits of penance. And again I declare to you that if, being ungrateful to God for His mercies, you return to your evil ways, your wounds shall open again, your punishment shall be twofold, and the wrath of God shall wax hotter against you than before." From that hour they began to do penance, in obedience to the holy man, and the cruel plagues which had molested them ceased, neither wolves nor hail troubling them again. And what is still more marvellous, when the hail fell on the neighboring fields, it stopped when it approached their boundaries, or fell upon other places. The hail having thus ceased, the wolves also kept the promise made by the servant of God, and ventured no more to rage against those men who no longer impiously rebelled against the laws of the merciful God. It behooves us, therefore, piously to venerate the piety of that blessed man, by whose marvellous sweetness and power ferocious beasts were quelled, wild animals tamed, and the nature of brutes, rebellious to man since his fall, was sweetly inclined to his obedience. For this virtue of piety it is which, uniting all things together, is profitable to all things, having the promise of this life and of that which is to come.

Chapter IX

OF THE FERVOR OF HIS CHARITY, AND OF HIS DESIRE OF MARTYRDOM.

HO can express the fervent charity which burnt in the heart of Francis, the friend of the Bridegroom? For he seemed to be absorbed, as a live coal in the furnace, in the flame of divine love. As soon as he heard the love of the Lord spoken of, he was moved, excited and inflamed, as if the chords of his heart within vibrated to the sound without. And he was wont to say that to offer this love of our heart as an alms was a noble prodigality, and that they were to be accounted most foolish who valued it less than money; for that the priceless worth of divine love was a sufficient purchase-money for the kingdom of Heaven, and that He who has so greatly loved us is greatly to be loved in return. Therefore, to excite himself by all things to divine love, he rejoiced in all the works of the Lord's hands, and, by the glory and beauty of that mirror, he arose to the principle and cause of them all. In all things fair he beheld Him Who is most fair, and by His footsteps in created things he found the way to his Beloved, making a ladder of all things by which to ascend to Him Who is to be desired above them all. With unspeakable devotion he enjoyed that fountain of goodness, flowing forth through all creatures as in so many streams; and perceiving a celestial harmony in the virtuous deeds offered in concert with them to God, after the manner of the prophet David, he sweetly exhorted them all to praise the Lord. He desired for

the exceeding ardor of his love, to be wholly transformed into Christ Jesus, Whom he laid, as a bundle
of myrrh, on his heart. Out of special devotion to Him,
he was accustomed to retire into a solitary and desert
place, and there to abide, from the feast of Epiphany
through the forty days which Christ spent in the desert.
There he remained shut up in his cell, praising God
without intermission, in continual prayer and the
utmost severity of abstinence. And as his love to Christ
was so fervent, so graciously was it returned by his
Beloved that, as the servant of God once revealed to
his familiar companion, his Saviour seemed to be almost
continually present before his eyes. His burning love
for the Sacrament of our Lord's Body seemed to con-
sume the very marrow of his bones, as he wondered
within himself which most to admire—the condescension of that charity, or the charity of that condescension of our Lord. He communicated often, and so
devoutly as to move others to devotion; and, by the
sweetness of that Immaculate Lamb, he was, as it were,
spiritually inebriated, and frequently rapt in ecstasy.
He bore unspeakable love to the Mother of our Lord
Jesus Christ, because by her the Lord of Majesty became
our Brother, and through her we have obtained mercy.
In her, next to Christ, he placed his confidence: he took
her for his advocate, and in her honor he was accustomed to fast devoutly, from the feast of the Apostles
Peter and Paul until the festival of the Assumption.
He was likewise bound to the Angelical Spirits by an
inseparable bond of affection, because by them the souls
of the elect are enkindled and raised to God by a marvellous fire of love; and therefore, in devotion to them,
he fasted forty days, from the feast of the Assumption
of the glorious Virgin, giving himself, for that time,
wholly to prayer. To the Blessed Michael the Archangel
he had a more special devotion; and he honored him

with peculiar love, because to him was committed the office of presenting souls to God. And this devotion came from his fervent zeal for the salvation of all the elect. When he remembered all the Saints, whom he was wont to call stones enkindled through and through with the fire of divine love, he was all inflamed with heavenly charity; and he honored with the highest degree of reverence and love the holy Apostles, and chiefly St. Peter and St. Paul, because of the love and reverence which they bore to Christ, and he dedicated a special Lent to the Lord in their honor.

Now, this poor man of Christ had but two pieces of money—to wit, his body and his soul—which in his liberal charity he could bestow upon others, and of these he made a continual offering for the love of Christ; for by his rigorous fasting, during almost the whole course of his life, he sacrificed his body to God; and likewise his spirit by the ardor of its desires; offering the holocaust in the outer court, and at the same time burning incense and most sweet odors on the altar within. And while the excessive devotion of his charity raised him to high and sublime things, so in his loving benignity he communicated himself to all those who were partakers of the same grace and nature with himself; for it is no marvel that he who, in the natural piety of his heart, accounted himself to be the fellow and the brother of all creatures, was drawn, by the charity of Christ, to a still closer union and brotherhood with them, when adorned with the likeness of his Creator and Redeemer. He would not have accounted himself to be the friend of Christ if he had been wanting in care for those souls who had been redeemed by His Blood. He was wont to say that nothing was to be preferred to the salvation of souls, and this he proved chiefly by the fact that the only begotten Son of God had vouchsafed to die upon the Cross for their redemption. This, therefore, was ever the object of his most fervent prayers; of this he continually discoursed in his sermons, and commended it by the force of his example. When he was sometimes reproved for his excessive austerity of life, he would reply that he was set forth as an example to others; and, indeed, his innocent flesh, which was ever willingly subject to the spirit, needed not the scourge for any offence of its own; yet, as an example to others, he loaded it with the burden of penance, leading a hard and austere life for their sake; for he said: "Though I should speak with the tongue of men and of angels, and have not charity, nor show to my neighbor an example of virtue, I should be of little service to him, and none to myself." And with this burning fire of charity he sought to imitate the glorious triumph of the martyrs in the inextinguishable flame of their love, and the invincible courage of their spirit; so that, in the perfect charity which casteth out fear, he offered himself to the Lord as a living sacrifice in the fire of martyrdom, thus to requite Him Who died for us, and to excite others to His divine love.

In the sixth year after his conversion, being thus all on fire with the desire of martyrdom, he determined to pass into Syria, to preach the Christian faith and penance to the Saracens and other infidels there. Having entered a ship in order to accomplish his desire, he was forced by contrary winds to land in the country of Sclavonia. Having remained there for some time, unable to find any ship to carry him whither he desired to go, he besought certain mariners who were bound for Ancona to carry him thither for the love of God, which they refusing, because he had not wherewithal to support himself during the voyage, the holy man, trusting fully in the goodness of God, secretly entered the ship with his companion, and hid himself there.

Forthwith there came a messenger from God to the aid of His poor servant, bringing him the necessary food for his voyage; and calling one of the sailors, who greatly feared God, he said to him: "Keep these things faithfully for the two poor friars who are hidden in this ship, and when the time of need shall come, supply them charitably therewith." When the ship had left the harbor, the sailors being prevented by contrary winds from touching at any port, their provisions were exhausted, and nothing remained but that which had been given in alms to the poor friars; and that which was very small in quantity increased in such measure by the power of God, that it sufficed for the necessities of the whole crew, who were kept at sea by stress of weather, and tempest-tossed for many days before they arrived at the harbor of Ancona. Then the sailors, seeing that by the merits of the servant of God they had passed through so many perils of death, having felt the terror of the tempest, and seeing the wonderful works of the Saint in the depths of the sea, gave thanks to Almighty God, Who shows Himself ever wonderful and loving in His servants and His friends. Having disembarked, he began to traverse the country, sowing the seed of salvation and gathering an abundant harvest.

But because his heart yearned after the fruit of martyrdom, desiring above all things a precious death for Christ, he took the road to Morocco, that he might preach the Gospel of Christ to the Miramolin and all his people, thinking thus to attain the palm for which he so fervently longed; and so was he carried forward by that desire, that, weak as he was in body, he far outstripped his companion in speed; and thus in haste and, as it were, in ecstasy of spirit, he seemed to fly rather than walk. But no sooner had he arrived in Spain than by the divine disposal, which reserved him for greater things, there fell upon him so grievous a sickness that he was unable to proceed according to his desire. The man of God, knowing, therefore, that his life in the flesh was necessary to the children whom he had brought forth in the spirit, although he accounted death to be a gain to himself, returned to feed the flock committed to his care.

But being urged in the spirit to martyrdom by the intense ardor of his charity, he sought a third time to spread the faith in the Holy Trinity by the shedding of his blood, and endeavored again to make his way to the land of the infidels. In the thirteenth year after his conversion he went into Syria, and boldly exposed himself to many dangers to gain admittance to the Sultan of Babylon. At that time so implacable a warfare was raging between the Christians and the Saracens, the armies of both nations being encamped over against each other, that it was impossible to pass from one to the other without peril of death. For the Sultan had made a cruel decree, that whoever should bring him the head of a Christian should receive a gold bezant as his reward. But Francis, the valiant soldier of Christ, hoping shortly to attain the end which he had set before him, determined to undertake the adventure, not terrified by the fear, but rather excited by the desire, of death. Having, then, prayed to the Lord, and being strengthened by Him, he sang with great confidence those words of the prophet, "Though I should walk in the midst of the shadow of death, I will fear no evil, for Thou art with me." He took with him, therefore, as his companion, a brother named Illuminatus— a man, indeed, of virtue and illumination—and on their way they met two sheep, which, when the holy man saw, he said to his companion, "My brother, trust in the Lord, for in us is fulfilled those words of the Gospel, 'Behold I send you forth as sheep in the midst of

wolves.'" When they had gone a little farther, they met
with a band of Saracens who, quickly falling upon them,
like wolves upon a flock of sheep, cruelly seized and
bound the servants of God, dealing fiercely and con-
temptuously with them, and with many vile words and
hard blows carried them along in cruel bonds. Lastly,
having in many ways afflicted and oppressed them,
they were by the divine disposal, and according to the
holy man's desire, brought into the presence of the Sultan. And being questioned by that prince whence and
for what purpose they had come, by whom they had
been sent, and by what means they had come thither,
Francis, the servant of God, made answer with a heart
void of fear, that they had been sent, not by man, but
by the Most High God, to show to him and his people
the way of salvation, and make known to them the
truth of the Gospel. And truly with such constancy of
mind, such fortitude of soul, and such fervor of spirit
did he preach to that Sultan One God in Three Persons, and Jesus Christ the Saviour of all men, that in
him was gloriously fulfilled that promise of the Gospel:
"I will give to you a mouth and wisdom, which none
of your adversaries shall be able to resist or contra-
dict." The Sultan, therefore, admiring the courage and
fervor of spirit which he beheld in the man of God, listened to him willingly, and earnestly besought him to
remain with him. But the servant of Christ, being
enlightened from on high, answered him thus: "If thou
and thy people will be converted to Christ, for His love
I will willingly abide with thee. But if thou art doubtful whether or not to forsake the law of Mahomed for
the faith of Christ, command a great fire to be lighted,
and I will go into it with thy priests, that it may be
known which faith should be held to be the most certain and the most holy." To whom the Sultan made
answer: "I do not believe that any of my priests would

be willing to expose himself to the fire, or to endure any manner of torment in defense of his faith." For he had just seen one of the most aged amongst his priests, and of greatest credit and authority, depart from his presence at the words which Francis had spoken. Then said the holy man: "If thou wilt promise me for thyself and thy people that thou wilt embrace the worship of Christ if I come forth unharmed, I will enter the fire alone. And if I shall be burnt, let it be imputed to my sins. But if the Divine Power shall protect me, then let all of you acknowledge Christ to be the Power and Wisdom of God, the true God and the Lord and Saviour of all men." But the Sultan answered that he dared not accept this challenge, because he feared a sedition of the people. Nevertheless he offered him many precious gifts, which the man of God, who coveted not worldly things, but sought only the salvation of souls, despised as so much dust. The Sultan, beholding in this holy man so perfect a contempt of all worldly things, was moved to admiration, and conceived a still greater veneration for him. And although he would not, or perhaps dared not, embrace the Christian faith, yet he devoutly besought the servant of Christ that he would receive the aforesaid gifts for his salvation, and either distribute them amongst the poor of Christ, or employ them in the building of churches. But he, who ever avoided the burden of money, and saw no root of true piety in the Sultan's soul, would by no means consent to his desire. Seeing, also, that he made no progress in the conversion of this people, nor could attain his desire of martyrdom, being admonished by divine revelation, he returned into the region of the faithful; the clemency of God thus ordaining most mercifully and marvelously, to the greater advance of the holy man in virtue, that this friend of Christ should seek death with all his power, and yet be unable to find it; that he should not want the merit of the martyrdom of the will, and yet should be preserved hereafter to receive the singular privilege of the Stigmata. And so it was that the fire of divine love was kindled more and more perfectly in his heart, till it was mightily manifested in his flesh. Oh, truly blessed man, who, if his flesh felt not the tyrant's steel, wanted not the likeness of the Lamb that was slain! Oh, truly and fully blessed, I say, who, if his life perished not under the sword of persecution, yet missed not the palm of martyrdom!

Chapter X

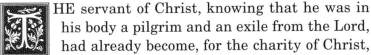

HE servant of Christ, knowing that he was in his body a pilgrim and an exile from the Lord, had already become, for the charity of Christ, wholly insensible to the desire of earthly or exterior things, lest he should remain without the consolation of true love; and so, praying without intermission, he endeavored to keep his spirit in the continual presence of God. And great, assuredly, was his consolation in prayer, while he contemplated the whole circle of the mansions of the angels, with whom he was already a fellow-citizen, and with fervent desires sought his Beloved, from whom he was only divided by the wall of the flesh. And this prayer was also a great help to him in all his works, wherein he distrusted his own endeavors; and trusting wholly in prayer, rested all his thoughts upon the Lord. He affirmed that a religious man ought to desire above every other gift the grace of prayer; and believing that without it no progress can be made in the service of God, he labored, by every means in his power, to excite his brethren to its exercise. Whether walking or sitting, at home or abroad, laboring or resting, he was ever intent on prayer, so that he seemed to have dedicated to it not only his heart and his body, and all that was in him, but also his work and his time. Neither was he ever accustomed negligently to pass over any spiritual visitation; but when it was offered to him he followed it, and as long as it was vouchsafed him by the Lord he enjoyed its sweetness: for if, when journeying in intense thought, he felt some good and divine inspiration, laying aside other thoughts, he dwelt upon this, turning the new inspiration to account so that he received not that grace in vain. He was often raised to such a height of contemplation as to be carried out of himself; and experiencing something beyond human sense, he became unconscious of what passed around him.

Passing through the town of Santo Sepulchro, a very populous place, riding upon an ass, because of the weakness of his body, he was surrounded by a great crowd, who gathered round him from devotion. Being pressed by the people on every side, he seemed to feel nothing any more than if he had been an inanimate corpse; he took no notice of anything around him, nor was he conscious of anything that was done; so that when he came to a hospital for poor lepers, which was on the other side of the town, as if awaking from his heavenly contemplations, he inquired anxiously whether they were near Santo Sepulchro. For his mind, always intent on the glories of Heaven, felt not the variation of places or times, or the presence of persons. And that this happened frequently is attested by the experience of many of his companions.

And having learnt in prayer that the desired presence of the Holy Ghost is enjoyed with greatest familiarity at a distance from the noise and distractions of the world, he sought out solitary places, making his nightly prayer in lonely and deserted churches. Here he often endured most horrible conflicts with the demons, who sensibly attacked him, endeavoring to disturb him in his prayer. But he, armed with celestial weapons, the more vehemently he was attacked by his enemies, had recourse the more fervently and earnestly to prayer, saying to the Lord: "Protect me under the shadow of Thy wings from the face of the wicked who afflict me." And then to the demons: "Do your worst, malignant and false spirits, for you can do nothing but what you are permitted to do by God; and I am ready to suffer with all joy whatsoever His divine goodness has decreed for me." And the proud demons, unable to endure this constancy of mind, retired in confusion. The man of God, remaining tranquil in his solitude, made the woods resound with his sighs, and bathed them with his tears. He beat his breast, and discoursed familiarly with his Lord. Here he made answer to Him as a judge, besought Him as a father, conversed with Him as a friend; and here he was often heard by the brethren, who piously observed him, imploring the divine clemency for sinners with great sighs and tears, and crying with a loud voice, as if the Passion of the Lord had been presented before his eyes; here he was seen praying all night long, with his arms extended in the form of a cross, his whole body being raised from the ground, and surrounded by a luminous cloud, so that the marvellous light which shone forth from his body bore glorious testimony to his wonderful illumination of mind. Here again, as was proved by manifest signs, all the uncertain and hidden things of the divine wisdom were revealed to him, which he divulged not to others, unless when the charity of Christ urged, and the profit of his neighbor required it. For he was wont to say that it is easy to lose for a little price a thing so precious that no price can purchase it, and thus to provoke the giver not to give it to us again.

When he returned from his private prayers, by which he was changed, as it were, into another man, he strove earnestly to conform himself to the manner of his companions, lest he should show outwardly that which he had experienced within, and thus lose the interior reward by exposing it to the air of man's admiration. When he received any visitation from the Lord in public, he endeavored to turn away the attention of the bystanders, lest the familiarity vouchsafed to him by his divine Spouse should be made known to the world. When he was in prayer with the brethren, he carefully avoided sighs, groans, or any exterior signs of emotion, whether because he loved secrecy, or because he was interiorly absorbed in the presence of God. He would often say to the brethren: "When a servant of God receives any divine inspiration in prayer, he ought to say, 'This consolation, O Lord, Thou hast sent from Heaven to me, a most unworthy sinner, and I commit it to Thy care, for I know that I should be but a thief of Thy treasure.' And when he returns to prayer, he ought to bear himself as a little one and a sinner, as if he had received no new grace from God."

It happened one day when the holy man was at the Portiuncula, the Bishop of Assisi came, as was his custom, to visit him; and when he came to the place passed on, with greater confidence than was befitting, to the cell where the servant of Christ was praying. He knocked at the door, and had no sooner put in his head than he beheld the holy man at prayer, and was immediately struck with terror; his hair stood on end, and all his limbs seemed to stiffen, so that he even lost the use of his speech, and was suddenly and forcibly driven backwards by the divine power to a great distance from the cell. The Bishop in amazement went to the brethren in such haste as he was able, and God having restored the use of his speech, his first word was to confess his fault.

Another time the Abbot of the Monastery of St. Justin, of the diocese of Perugia, met the servant of Christ. As soon as he saw him, the devout Abbot dismounted in haste, that he might do reverence to the man of God, and confer with him concerning the salvation of souls. After this sweet conference, the Abbot took his leave, humbly beseeching Francis to pray for him. The man dear to God replied, "I will willingly pray for thee." A little while after the Abbot's departure, the faithful Francis said to his companion: "Wait awhile, brother, until I fulfill the promise which I have made." Now, while he was praying, the Abbot suddenly felt an unusual fervor and sweetness in his spirit, so that he was wrapped in ecstasy of mind, and wholly dissolved in God. When he came to himself, he recognized the power of the prayer of St. Francis. From that moment he conceived an increased love for the Order, and related the fact as a miracle to many persons.

The holy man was accustomed to recite the Canonical Hours with the greatest reverence and devotion. For although he suffered from weakness of the eyes, the stomach, the spleen, and the liver, yet while he said the Office he would never lean against the wall, but always stood erect and bare-headed, without wandering of the eye or any other interruption. And when he was travelling he always stopped to say the Office, nor did he ever omit this holy and devout custom, however inclement the weather or abundant the rain. For he said: "If quiet is needed to eat the bread of the body, which, with what it eats, shall become the food of worms, with how far greater peace and tranquillity ought the soul to receive the nourishment of its life!"

He accounted it a great offence if, at the time of prayer, he was distracted by any vain fancies. If any such thing befell him, he failed not immediately to expiate it by confession. And by this continual watchfulness it happened that he was rarely troubled by flies of this kind. It happened one Lent that he had made a certain vessel, in order to occupy his time, so that not the slightest portion of it might be lost. As he was saying Tierce this work came into his memory, and distracted his mind for a moment. In fervor of spirit, he took the little vessel, and cast it into the fire, saying, "I will sacrifice to the Lord that which has hindered His sacrifice." He recited the Psalms with such intention of mind and spirit, as if he had God present with him; and whenever the Name of the Lord occurred in them, it seemed to leave a sensible sweetness on his lips. In order that the Name of the Lord, not only in thought, but in speech or writing, should be fitly honored, he persuaded the brethren, whenever they found any written papers, to lay them up carefully in some fitting place, lest perhaps the sacred Name therein contained might be trodden under foot. Whenever he spoke or heard the Name of Jesus, the joy which filled him interiorly was manifestly seen in his exterior, even as if he tasted some sweet savor, or some harmonious sound filled his ear.

It happened in the third year before his death, that in order to excite the inhabitants of Grecio to commemorate the nativity of the Infant Jesus with great devotion, he determined to keep it with all possible solemnity; and lest he should be accused of lightness or novelty, he asked and obtained the permission of the sovereign Pontiff. Then he prepared a manger, and brought hay, and an ox and an ass to the place appointed. The brethren were summoned, the people ran together, the forest resounded with their voices, and that venerable night was made glorious by many and brilliant lights and sonorous psalms of praise. The man of God stood before the manger, full of devotion and piety, bathed in tears and radiant with joy; many Masses were said before it, and the Holy Gospel was chanted by Francis, the Levite of Christ. Then he preached to the people around of the nativity of the poor King; and being unable to utter his Name for the tenderness of his love, he called Him the Babe of Bethlehem. A certain valiant and veracious soldier, Master

John of Grecio, who, for the love of Christ, had left the warfare of this world, and become a dear friend of the holy man, affirmed that he beheld an Infant marvelously beautiful sleeping in that manger, Whom the blessed Father Francis embraced with both his arms, as if he would awake Him from sleep. This vision of the devout soldier is credible, not only by reason of the sanctity of him that saw it, but by reason of the miracles which afterwards confirmed its truth. For the example of Francis, if it be considered by the world, is doubtless sufficient to excite all hearts which are negligent in the faith of Christ; and the hay of that manger, being preserved by the people, miraculously cured all diseases of cattle, and many other pestilences; God thus in all things glorifying His servant, and witnessing to the great efficacy of his holy prayers by manifest prodigies and miracles.

Chapter XI

OF HIS KNOWLEDGE OF HOLY SCRIPTURE, AND OF HIS
SPIRIT OF PROPHECY.

THIS incredible and unremitting exercise of prayer, together with the continual practice of all virtues, had already brought the holy man to such serenity of mind that, although he had no knowledge of the Scriptures by human teaching, nevertheless, being illuminated by the splendor of the eternal light, he investigated with marvellous acuteness of mind all the most profound secrets of the sacred writings, because his understanding, being purified from every stain, penetrated the most hidden things of the holy mysteries; and where theological science enters not, but remains without, thither entered the affection of the lover of God. He read continually the sacred books, and what had once entered his mind he retained firmly in his memory. For he received not in vain with the ear of mental attention, that which he continually dwelt upon with tender devotion. Being once asked by the brethren whether it was his pleasure that learned men who entered his Order should apply themselves to the study of the Holy Scriptures, he replied, "Assuredly it pleases me that while they follow the example of Christ, of whom we read that He gave Himself more to prayer than to reading, they should not, on that account, neglect the study of prayer. Nevertheless, I would not have them study in order to know how they ought to speak, but in order that they may do the things which they hear, and when they have done them, that they may set them before others. I would," said he, "have my friars to be disciples of the Gospel, and so to increase in the knowledge of the truth, that they may grow, at the same time, in purity and simplicity, so that they may not separate from the wisdom of the serpent the simplicity of the dove, which our Divine Master joined together with His blessed mouth." When he was at Siena, he was asked by a pious man, a doctor in theology, some questions of great difficulty; and he opened the secrets of the divine wisdom with so much clearness, that this learned man marvelled greatly. He afterwards said that truly the theology of that holy Father rose like a soaring eagle upon the two wings of purity and contemplation, whereas, said he, "our science grovels like a serpent in the dust." For although he was rude in speech, he was, nevertheless, so full of holy wisdom that he could solve all doubtful questions, and disclose all hidden mysteries. Nor is it surprising that the holy man had received from God the understanding of the Holy Scriptures, seeing that, imitating Christ in His life and His works, he bore engraven upon his heart the image of that Divine Teacher by Whom they were dictated.

So fully did he possess the spirit of prophecy, that he foretold things to come, and beheld the secrets of hearts, and knew things absent as if they were present, and showed himself in a marvellous manner to those that were afar off. For at the time that the Christian hosts were besieging the city of Damietta, the holy man was there, not armed with the armor of this world, but with the weapons of faith. The day appointed for a battle having arrived, and the Christians preparing for the conflict, the servant of God, when he heard of it, began to weep bitterly, and said to his companion, "If these fight today, the Lord hath revealed to me that our Christians shall not prevail; but if I tell them so,

I shall be accounted a fool, and if I keep silence, my conscience will reproach me. What thinkest thou that I ought to do?" And his companion made answer: "Brother, trouble not thyself because of the judgments of men, for it will not be the first time that thou hast been accounted a fool; discharge thy conscience, therefore, and fear God rather than men." When he had heard these words, the messenger of Christ went forth and spoke to the Christians a salutary admonition, forbidding them to fight, and foretelling their overthrow; but when the soldiers heard his words they mocked at them, accounting them to be vain fables, and so hardened their hearts that they would in nowise desist from their purpose. They engaged in a battle with the enemy, and after a severe conflict the whole Christian chivalry was put to flight, receiving shame and contempt instead of victory; and so great was the slaughter and the overthrow, that the Christians lost about six thousand men, either made prisoners or slain. Whereby it plainly appeared that the wisdom of the poor Francis was not to be despised, inasmuch as the soul of the just man sees and declares the truth more plainly than seven watchmen set upon their tower.

At another time, after his return from beyond the sea, he went to Celano to preach, and a certain soldier besought him with great devotion that he would eat with him. When the holy man came into the soldier's house all the family rejoiced greatly to receive this poor one of the Lord. And before he began to eat, according to his custom, the holy man offered his usual prayers and praises to God, with his eyes raised to Heaven. When he had finished his prayer, he familiarly called his kind host aside, and said to him: "Behold, my host and brother, in compliance with thy prayers I have come to eat in thy house. But now attend to that which I say to thee, for thou shalt no more eat here, but elsewhere. Therefore, confess thy sins with truly penitent contrition; let nothing remain in thee unrevealed by true confession, for the Lord will requite thee today for the kindness with which thou hast received His poor servant." The good man believed these holy words, and disclosing all his sins in confession to the companion of St. Francis, he set all his house in order, making himself ready for death, and preparing himself for it to the best of his power. They then sat down to table, and the others began to eat, but the spirit of the host immediately departed, according to the words of the man of God, which foretold his sudden death. And so it came to pass that by the merit of his hospitality, he who, in the words of truth, had received a prophet, received also a prophet's reward; for by the prophetical warning of the holy man this devout soldier was provided against sudden death, inasmuch as, fortified by the arms of penance, he escaped eternal damnation, and entered the kingdom of Heaven.

When the holy man was lying sick at Rieti, a certain prebendary, named Gedeon, a vain and worldly man, was attacked by a grievous sickness; and causing himself to be carried in his bed to the holy man, he and all those present besought him with tears to make the sign of the Cross over him. But the holy man replied: "Thou hast lived until now according to the desires of the flesh, nor hast thou ever feared the judgments of God; wherefore, then, wouldst thou have me sign thee with the sign of the Cross? Nevertheless, because of the devout prayers of these who intercede for thee, I will sign thee with the Cross in the Name of the Lord. But know this, that if, after thou shalt be delivered, thou return to thy evil ways, thou shalt suffer far greater torments than these." He signed him, therefore, with the Cross: and immediately he, whose limbs had been all contracted, arose in perfect health, and breaking forth into the praises of God, he cried: "I am free;" and at the same instant his bones seemed to crack, as when dry wood is broken by the hand, and that sound was heard by all present. But after a short time had passed, he forgot God, and returned again to his sins. When supping one evening at the house of a certain canon, where he was to sleep that night, the roof of the house suddenly fell in; and all the rest who were within it having escaped, that miserable man remained there alone, and was killed on the spot. Thus, by the just judgment of God, a worse evil than the first befell that wicked man, by reason of his ingratitude and contempt of God; whence we may learn to be thankful for pardon once received, for the guilt is twofold of sin committed after a fresh benefit has been bestowed.

Another time, a certain noble lady, who was very devout to God, came to the holy man to lay before him a trouble under which she was suffering, and to ask him for a remedy. She had a husband, who was exceedingly cruel, and who hindered her in the service of Christ; and therefore she besought the holy man to pray for her, that God, of His clemency, would soften her husband's heart. "Go in peace," said the man of God; "for in a short time thou shalt receive consolation from thy husband." And he added: "Tell him from God and from me that now is the time of mercy; soon it shall be the time of justice." The lady, having received his blessing, returned home, and gave her message to her husband. Then the Holy Spirit fell upon him, and made him a new man, so that he answered her mildly, "Lady, let us serve the Lord, and save our souls." And so, by persuasion of his holy wife, they both led for many years a life of celibacy; and then, on the same day, they departed together to the Lord.

Marvellous, assuredly, was the prophetical power in the holy man, by which he restored strength to dry and withered limbs, and infused piety into the hardest hearts; and no less marvellous was the illumination of his spirit, by which he foresaw future events, and penetrated the secrets of the conscience, having, like another Eliseus, received a double portion of the spirit of Elias. For having predicted at Siena, to a certain friend of his, things which were to happen to him hereafter, that learned man, of whom we have spoken before, who often conferred with him concerning the Holy Scriptures, and who had heard of this prediction, asked the holy Father whether he had indeed foretold these things before they happened. He not only affirmed that he had so spoken, but at the same time predicted the end of him who was now inquiring concerning what had happened to another and, to impress the prediction more deeply on his heart, he revealed to him a secret scruple of conscience of which that learned man had never spoken to anyone, leading him to lay it fully open, and then explaining it and giving him loving counsel thereupon, to his great edification and amazement. In confirmation of all these things aforesaid, we may add that this religious ended his life exactly as the servant of Christ had foretold.

At the time when he had just returned from beyond seas, having with him, as his companion, Brother Leonard of Assisi, being overcome with weariness, he rode for awhile on an ass; and as his companion, who was also exceedingly weary, followed him, he began to say within himself (being overcome by human weakness), "His parents were no equals of mine, and behold he is riding, and I am leading his ass on foot."

As this thought passed through the mind of Brother Leonard, the holy man immediately dismounted from the ass and said, "It is not fitting, brother, that I should ride and thou shouldst walk, because thou wast nobler and mightier in the world than I." When the brother heard this, he was full of shame and wonder, and coming to himself, he threw himself at the feet of the holy man and plainly acknowledged his fault, asking pardon for it.

There was a certain friar, very devout to God and to Francis, the servant of Christ, who frequently thought within himself how worthy of divine favor was the holy man, by whom he was also affectionately and familiarly beloved, while he was possessed by the thought that he was himself a castaway, and excluded from the number of the elect. Being frequently, therefore, assailed by this thought, he greatly desired the familiarity of the servant of God. Yet he revealed to none the secret of his heart, till the holy man, calling this friar to him one day, began thus sweetly to speak to him: "My son, suffer not thyself to be troubled by such thoughts as these, for I hold thee most dear, and number thee among those I love best, and freely bestow upon thee my familiarity and friendship." The brother, in astonishment, became still more devout to the holy Father than he was before, and not only increased in his love to him, but was enriched by the grace of the Holy Spirit with many and wonderful gifts.

Being one day shut up in his cell on the mountain of Alvernia, one of the holy Father's companions greatly desired some short note on the Word of God, written by his hand. For he firmly believed that thereby he should be set free from a grievous temptation, not of the flesh, but of the spirit, under which he was now suffering severely, or at least be able more easily to endure it. Being then molested with this desire, he was greatly troubled in mind, because he was ashamed to reveal his thoughts to the holy and reverend Father. But although he would not tell it to him, it was revealed to him by the Spirit of God; therefore he commanded the said friar to bring him ink and paper, and thereupon he wrote with his own hand certain praises of the Lord, according to his brother's desire, and then gave it to him with his blessing, saying: "Take this paper and keep it diligently, even to the day of thy death." The brother took the desired gift, and immediately that temptation departed from him. He kept the writing, which remains until this day, and by it have many marvellous things been wrought in testimony of the power of St. Francis.

There was another friar who appeared outwardly to be a man of great sanctity and exemplary life, yet of great singularity. He spent all his time in prayer, and observed silence so strictly that he would not even confess in words, but only by signs. It happened that the holy Father Francis came to see this brother, and to speak concerning him with the other friars. When they all praised and extolled him, the man of God replied: "Be silent, brethren, and praise not to me the diabolical delusion under which he labors. For know, in truth, that this is a diabolical temptation and a fraudulent deception." The brethren thought these words very severe, accounting it impossible that any fraud or delusion should be mixed with what they accounted so perfect. But not many days passed before the said friar left the Order, when it plainly appeared with what clearness and interior penetration the man of God had pierced to the very secrets of his heart. In the same way he foresaw the ruin of many who appeared likely to persevere; and, on the contrary, predicted with assured certainty the conversion of many sinners to Christ, so that it appeared that he was very near to the contemplation of that clear mirror of Divine and Eternal Truth, Whose marvellous splendor lighted up for him those things from which he was far distant in the body, so that he discerned them with his mental eye as if they were actually present.

His vicar one day holding chapter in his place, while he was praying in his cell, he was, as it were, a mediator between his brethren and God. For it happened that one of the brethren, making an idle excuse for some error which he had committed, would not submit to holy discipline, which the holy man beholding in spirit, he called one of the friars to him, and said: "I have seen the devil sitting on the shoulders of that disobedient friar, who, under the guidance of such a rider, thus holding him tight by the neck, turns hither and thither whithersoever he guides him. But I have prayed to God for the brother, and the devil departs in confusion. Go, therefore, and say to that friar that he submit his neck at once to the yoke of holy obedience." And the brother, being admonished by the messenger, immediately returned to God, and fell humbly at the feet of the vicar.

It happened at another time, that two friars came from distant parts to the hermitage of Grecio, to see the man of God and receive his benediction, which they had long greatly desired. They came, therefore, and found him not, for he had just returned from the monastery to his cell, so they were going desolate away. And behold, as they were departing, the holy man, who had no human means of knowing either their coming or their departure, contrary to his usual custom, came forth from his cell and called after them and blessed them, according to their desire, in the Name of Christ, with the sign of the Cross.

Another day, two brethren came together from a place called Lavora, the elder of whom gave some scandal to the younger. And when they came to the holy man, he asked the younger how his companion had borne himself on the way. When he replied, "Very well,"—"Take heed, brother," said he, "lest thou tell a lie under the semblance of humility, for I know what

I know: but wait awhile and thou shalt see." The brother was greatly astonished how he came thus to know absent things by the spirit. But not many days afterwards he who had given scandal to the other departed in contempt of religion, having neither asked pardon of the Father, nor submitted himself to the correction of due discipline. So that in the ruin of this one man two things were made manifest—the divine justice, and the prophetical spirit of St. Francis. And that, by the divine power, he showed himself present to the absent is manifest by what has been already said. Be it remembered also, that when absent he appeared to the brethren transfigured in a fiery chariot, and at the Chapter of Arles presented himself in the form of a Cross. And this was done, we may believe, by the divine disposal, in order that by the marvellous apparition of his bodily presence might be plainly manifested the presence of his spirit, with the light of Eternal Wisdom, light being the swiftest of all things that move, and by its pureness and clearness infusing itself into holy souls in all nations of the world, thus making them the friends and the prophets of God. The Heavenly Teacher is wont to manifest His mysteries to simple and humble men, as he showed in David, the most excellent of all the prophets; and afterwards in Peter, the prince of all the Apostles; and lastly in Francis, the poor little servant of Christ. For they, being simple, and ignorant of human learning, were made by the Holy Spirit illustrious for their erudition. The shepherd was taken from feeding his flock to lead the people of God out of Egypt; the fisherman was called to fill the net of the Church with a multitude of believers; the merchant, to sell and scatter all things for Christ, that he might buy the pearl of evangelical perfection.

Chapter XII

OF THE EFFICACY OF HIS PREACHING, AND OF HIS GIFT
OF HEALING.

RANCIS, the true servant and minister of Christ, in order that he might perform all his works with the greatest fidelity and perfection, exercised himself chiefly in those virtues which he knew by the teaching of the Holy Spirit to be most pleasing to God. Now, it happened that he was once seized with great anguish of mind from a doubt as to what he ought to do, which, after spending many days in prayer, he laid before some of the brethren in whom he most confided "Which, my brethren," he said, "do you account most praiseworthy, which do you advise me to do—to give myself wholly to prayer, or to go about preaching the Gospel? For I, being a poor sinful man, and unskilled in preaching, have received the gift of prayer, rather than of speech. In prayer, again, is great gain and accumulation of graces; in preaching, the distribution of whatever gifts we have received from Heaven. In prayer is the purification of the interior affections, and union with One True and Supreme God, together with an increase of all virtues. In preaching, the feet of the spiritual man are defiled with dust; therewith comes distraction concerning many things and great relaxation of discipline. In prayer we speak with God, and listen to Him, and, as if leading an angelic life, we converse with angels. But in preaching we must condescend to men in many things; and living among them as men, we must think, see, speak, and hear as men. On the other hand, this one thing would seem to outweigh all the rest before God, viz., that the Only Begotten Son of God, Who is the Supreme Wisdom, descended from the bosom of the Father for the salvation of souls, that He might teach the world by His example, and speak the word of salvation to men whom He redeemed with the price of His sacred Blood, washing them therewith in the laver of Baptism, and nourishing them therewith in the Chalice of Salvation, reserving to Himself nothing, but pouring forth all liberally for our salvation. And therefore we ought to do according to the example of those things which we have seen in Him, as in a high mountain set forth before us, so that it seems to me more pleasing to God that I should lay aside my quiet, and go forth to labor."

Now, for many days together he pondered over these things with the brethren, and yet was unable to perceive certainly which of these two things he should do, and which would be most acceptable to Christ. For although he knew wonderful things by the spirit of prophecy, yet he was unable of himself clearly to resolve this question, God in His wisdom thus providing that the merit of preaching should be more plainly manifested by a divine revelation, and the humility of the servant of Christ might be at the same time preserved. It was ever his chief care to inquire in what way and by what means God might be most perfectly served according to His divine good pleasure. This was the sum of his philosophy, this his chief desire as long as he lived, to seek from the learned and the simple, the perfect and the imperfect, the little and the great, whatsoever might enable him to attain to the sublimest perfection of virtue. Calling, therefore, two of the brethren, he sent them to Brother Sylvester, who once beheld a Cross issuing from his mouth, and who now devoted himself to prayer in a mountain near Assisi, beseeching him that he would inquire the Divine Will concerning this thing, and make it known to him from the Lord. He asked the same thing of the holy virgin Clare, begging that she would cause some of the purest and simplest of her sisters to join with her in prayer, that so they might learn the Will of the Lord. The venerable priest and the virgin consecrated to God gave an answer in wonderful accordance, saying that it was revealed to them from on high to be the good pleasure of God that the servant of Christ should go forth to preach. The two brethren returning and making known the Will of God, as they had heard it, he immediately girded himself, and without any delay went forth on his way. He hastened with such fervor to fulfill the divine command, as if the hand of God upon him had endued him with strength from on High.

When he drew near to Bevagna, he came to a place where a great multitude of birds of different kinds were assembled together, which, when they saw the holy man, came swiftly to the place, and saluted him as if they had the use of reason. They all turned towards him and welcomed him; those which were on the trees bowed their heads in an unaccustomed manner, and all looked earnestly at him, until he went to them and seriously admonished them to listen to the word of the Lord, saying: "Oh, my brother birds, you are bound greatly to praise your Creator, Who has clothed you with feathers, and given you wings wherewith to fly; Who has given you the pure air for your dwelling-place, and governs and cares for you without any care of your own." While he spoke these and other such words to them, the bird's rejoiced in a marvellous manner, swelling their throats, spreading their wings, opening their beaks, and looking at him with great attention. And he, with marvellous fervor of spirit, passing through the midst of them, covered them with his tunic, neither did any one of them move from his place until the man of God had made the sign of the Cross and dismissed them with his blessing, when they all at once flew away. And all these things were seen by his companions, who were waiting for him on the road. When this pure and simple man returned to them, he began to accuse himself of negligence, because he had never before preached to the birds.

Afterwards, as he was preaching in the neighboring places, he came to a city called Alviano, where the people were gathered together, and there he silenced the swallows, who made their nests in that place, because for the great noise they made he could hardly be heard. Then the man of God said to them in the hearing of all: "My sisters, the swallows, it is now time that I also should speak, for you have spoken more than enough. Listen to the word of God, and keep silence until the preaching is ended." Then, as if they were capable of understanding, the swallows kept silence, and uttered not a sound until the sermon was ended. All who beheld this, being filled with wonder, glorified God. The fame of this miracle, being spread far and wide, greatly increased the reverence and faith borne to the man of God.

In the city of Paris there was a certain scholar of very good dispositions, who, with some of his companions, was diligently pursuing his studies. Being one day greatly troubled by the vexatious garrulity of a swallow, he said to his companions: "This must be one of the swallows which molested the holy man Francis while he was preaching, and would not desist until he had imposed silence upon them." Then turning to the swallow, he said confidently: "I command thee, in the name of Francis, the servant of God, to come to me, and I will quickly quiet thee." When the bird heard the name of Francis, as if it had been taught by the man of God, it was quiet at once, and came and placed itself in the scholar's hands, who in great amazement set it at liberty, and was troubled no more by its clamor.

At another time, when the servant of God was preaching at Gaeta, on the sea-shore, a multitude of people pressed upon him that they might touch him. The servant of Christ, who held such popular applause in abhorrence, entered alone a little boat which was close to the shore. And the boat, as if it had been a reasonable creature, was carried by an interior motion away from the shore, all who beheld it wondering, seeing that there was no one to row it. Having been carried some distance into the deep sea, it stopped, and remained immovable, while the holy man preached to the multitude who were waiting on the shore. Having heard the sermon and seen the miracle, the multitude received his blessing and retired, troubled him no more, and then the boat returned of itself to the land. Who could have been so obstinate and hardened in mind as to despise the preaching of Francis, by whose marvellous power it came to pass that not only irrational creatures, but inanimate substances, obeyed his words, as if they had been endowed with a soul!

Certain it is that with Francis, the servant of God, whithersoever he went there was ever present that Spirit of the Lord, Who had sent him forth; and the power and wisdom of Christ were with him, making him to abound in words of true and wholesome doctrine, and glorifying him with mighty miracles. For his word was as a burning fire, penetrating the inmost heart, and filling the minds of men with admiration, inasmuch as he sought after no ornaments of human invention, but showed forth only the divine inspiration and doctrine.

Having to preach on a certain day before the Pope

and the cardinals, at the suggestion of the Cardinal of Ostia he learned a sermon by heart, which he had very carefully prepared; when he was about to speak it for their edification he wholly forgot everything he had to say, so that he could not utter a word. He related with true humility what had befallen him, and then, having invoked the aid of the Holy Spirit, he began at once to move the hearts of these great men to compunction with such fluency of powerful and efficacious words, as plainly showed that not he, but the Spirit of the Lord, was speaking. And because he had first impressed upon his own mind by his works what he endeavored to impress upon others by his words, fearing reproof from no man, he preached the truth with great confidence. He was not accustomed to handle the sins of man delicately, but pierced them with the sword of the Spirit, nor did he spare their sinful lives, but rebuked them sharply and boldly. He spoke to great and small with equal constancy of mind, and with a like joyfulness of spirit, whether to many or to few; people of every age and sex came forth to see this man, newly given to the world by God, to look upon him and to listen to his words. And so he went forth through divers regions, boldly preaching the Gospel, the Lord working with him and confirming his word by signs following. And in the power of His Name, Francis, the herald of the truth, cast forth devils, healed the sick, and, what is more, by the efficacy of his word softened the most hardened hearts and brought them to penance, restoring at the same time the health of the body and the soul, as is shown by many of his works which we will notice, as a proof of what we have said.

In the city of Tuscanella he lodged with a certain soldier, who had devoutly besought him to do so. This soldier had an only son, whose limbs had been contracted from his birth. At the father's earnest request, the holy man raised him up with his hand, and thus, in the presence of all, restored him to health, so that all the members of his body were strengthened, and the child immediately began to walk, leaping and praising God.

In the city of Narni, at the desire of the Bishop, he made the sign of the Cross upon a paralytic who had lost the use of his limbs, and restored him to perfect health.

In the diocese of Rieti, a boy, whose body had for four years been swollen to such a degree that he could not see his legs, was brought by his mother, with many tears, to the holy man, and was immediately cured by the touch of his sacred hands.

In the city of Orti there was a boy so dreadfully distorted that he had his head between his feet, and many of his bones were broken. At the prayer of his parents the Blessed Francis signed him with the sign of the Cross, and immediately he was able to extend his limbs, and was delivered from his infirmity.

A woman in the city of Gubbio had both her hands contracted and withered, so that she was unable to use them. When the holy man had made the sign of the Cross over her, in the Name of the Lord, she recovered such perfect health that, like Simon's mother-in-law, who was healed by our Lord, she arose and prepared food for the use of the holy man and the poor.

In the city of Bevagna he thrice anointed a blind maiden with his spittle, in the Name of the Holy Trinity, and thus restored her sight.

A blind woman in the city of Narni recovered her sight when the holy man signed her with the sign of the Cross.

In Bologna there was a boy, one of whose eyes was so darkened by a spot that he could see nothing, nor could any remedy effect his cure. When the servant of

God had made the sign of the Cross over him from head to foot, he so perfectly recovered his sight that he soon after entered the Order of Friars Minor, and declared that he saw better with the eye which had been blind than with the other.

In the city of St. Emignano the servant of God was entertained by a devout man, whose wife was vexed by a devil. After he had prayed, he commanded the spirit by virtue of holy obedience to depart, and by the divine power so instantly cast him out, as plainly to manifest that the perversity of the demon cannot resist the power of holy obedience.

In the city of Castello a furious and malignant spirit, who had entered into a woman, having received an obedience from the holy man, departed in great wrath, leaving the woman whom he had possessed free both in body and mind.

One of the friars was possessed with so dreadful a sickness that by many it was affirmed to be rather the effect of diabolical art and malice than of natural infirmity. For he often threw himself at full length on the ground, and wallowed foaming; sometimes all the members of his body were contracted, sometimes distended, sometimes turned and twisted; now they would became rigid and hard, at other times his whole body would become stiff and distended, and he would rise with his feet upwards into the air, and fall down again in a horrible manner. Seeing therefore this unhappy man thus miserably and hopelessly tormented, the servant of Christ, being full of compassion, sent him a mouthful of bread which he was accustomed to eat, which the sick man had no sooner tasted than he received such strength that from that day forward he was never again troubled by his infirmity.

In the country of Arezzo a woman had been long laboring in childbirth, and was near to death, nor did any hope of life remain, save in the mercy of God. It happened that the servant of God was then passing through those parts, and from a weakness of body being compelled to ride, the horse upon which he had ridden was brought into the town where the woman lay sick. The men of the place, when they saw the horse upon which the holy man had ridden, took off the bridle and laid it upon the woman, and at its miraculous touch she was freed from all peril, and brought forth her child in safety.

A certain man of Pieve, full of piety and the fear of God, kept a cord by him which the holy Father had worn. A great multitude of men and women being attacked in the city by various diseases, he went from house to house where the sick lay, and dipping the cord in water, made the sick to drink thereof, by which means a great many were healed. Many sick persons, also, having eaten pieces of bread which had been touched by the man of God, were by the operation of the divine power speedily restored to health.

The herald of Christ being thus glorified by these and many other miracles, men listened to the things which he said in his preaching, as if an angel of the Lord were speaking to them. And forasmuch as he excelled in the possession of all virtues—in the spirit of prophecy; in the power of miracles; in the gift of preaching given him from Heaven; in the obedience rendered him by creatures without reason; in the mighty change of hearts at the hearing of his word; in the learning (beyond all human teaching to bestow) imparted to him by the Holy Ghost; in the authority to preach committed to him by divine revelation, by the Supreme Pontiff; in the rule wherein his manner of preaching was expressed, confirmed by the Vicar of Christ; finally,by the royal signet impressed upon his body—by all these tenfold witnesses, the venerable office, authentic doctrine, and wonderful sanctity of Francis, the herald of Christ, are undoubtedly proved, and he is set forth as the true messenger of God, declaring the Gospel of Christ.

Chapter XIII

OF THE SACRED STIGMATA.

T was the manner of this angelic man, Francis, never to rest from good works, but rather, like the heavenly spirits on Jacob's ladder, to be either ascending to God or descending to his neighbor. And he so prudently divided the time allotted him here for merit, that he spent the one part of it in labors for the good of his neighbor, and devoted the other to tranquil contemplation. Therefore, after descending to labor for the salvation of men, according to the exigency of time and place, he would leave behind him the tumult of the multitude, and retiring into some secret place where he might wait freely upon God, he would endeavor to purify his spirit from any dust which might have adhered to it in his conversation with men. Two years, therefore, before he gave up his spirit to God, he was led by Divine Providence, after manifold labors, into a mountainous place, which is called Mount Alvernia. Having there begun his fast, according to his wonted custom of keeping a Lent in honor of St. Michael the Archangel, being filled more abundantly than usual with divine sweetness by the contemplation of heavenly things, and enkindled by a more fervent desire of the things of God, he began to experience the gifts of the divine visitation more perfectly and abundantly than ever before. His spirit rose on high, not curiously to scrutinize the Divine Majesty, and so to be overwhelmed with its glory, but as a faithful and prudent servant seeking out the good pleasure of God, to which with the utmost ardor of love he desired to conform himself. It was infused, therefore, into his mind by divine inspiration that it should be revealed to him by Christ, on opening the Book of the Gospels, what in him, or from him, should be most acceptable to God. Having first prayed with great devotion, he therefore took the holy Book of the Gospels from the altar, and caused his companion, a devout and holy man, to open it thrice in the name of the Holy Trinity. Seeing that the book opened each time at the Passion of our Lord, the man of God understood that, as he had imitated Christ in the actions of his life, so, before he should depart from this world, he was to be conformed to Him likewise in the sufferings and pains of His Passion. And although, by the great austerity of his past life and his continual bearing of the Cross of Christ, he had become very feeble in body, yet was he not terrified, but prepared himself with good courage to endure the martyrdom set before him. For there grew in him an invincible fire of the love of his good Jesus, even a flame of burning charity, which many waters could not quench. Being thus raised to God by the ardor of seraphical love, and wholly transformed by the sweetness of compassion into Him, Who, of His exceeding charity, was pleased to be crucified for us; early in the morning of the Feast of the Exaltation of the Holy Cross, as he was praying in a secret and solitary place on the mountain, he beheld a seraph, having six wings, all on fire, descending to him from the height of Heaven. And as he flew with great swiftness towards the man of God, there appeared between the wings the form of One crucified, having His hands and feet stretched out and fixed to the Cross. Two wings rose above the head, two were stretched forth in flight, and two veiled the whole body. When he beheld this, he marvelled greatly, and his heart was filled with mingled joy and sorrow.

For he rejoiced at the gracious aspect with which Christ, under the form of the Seraph, looked upon him; yet to behold Him thus fastened to the Cross pierced his soul like a sword of compassion and grief. He wondered greatly at the appearance of so new and marvellous a vision, knowing that the infirmity of the Passion could in no wise agree with the immortality of the seraphical spirit. Lastly, he understood, by the revelation of the Lord, that this vision had been presented to his eyes by Divine Providence, that the friend of Christ might know that he was to be transformed into Christ crucified, not by the martyrdom of the flesh, but by the fire of the spirit. The vision, disappearing, left behind it a marvellous fire in his heart, and a no less wonderful sign impressed on his flesh. For there began immediately to appear in his hands and in his feet the appearance of nails, as he had now seen them in the vision of the Crucified. His hands and his feet appeared pierced through the midst with nails, the heads of the nails being seen in the insides of the hands and the upper part of the feet, and the points on the reverse side. The heads of the nails in the hands and feet were round and black, and the points somewhat long and bent, as if they had been turned back. On the right side, as if it had been pierced by a lance, was the mark of a red wound, from which the sacred blood often flowed, and stained his tunic. The servant of God, seeing the Stigmata thus deeply impressed on his flesh, so that he could not conceal them from his familiar companions, and yet fearing to discover the secret of the Lord, was in great trouble and perplexity whether he should declare or conceal what he had seen. He therefore called some of the brethren, and in general terms proposed his doubt to them, and asked their counsel. Then a certain friar, *Illuminates,* both by grace and by name, knowing that the holy man had seen some marvellous vision which had thus amazed him, answered: "Brother, not only for thine own sake, but for the sake of others, thou knowest the divine mysteries are made known to thee. And therefore it seems to me that thou shouldst fear to conceal this which thou hast received for the benefit of many, lest thou shouldst be condemned for hiding the talent committed to thy care." At these words, the holy man was so greatly moved, that though he was accustomed to say on these occasions, "Secretum meum mihi"—My secret is to myself—he now related with great fear all the order of the aforesaid vision, adding that He Who had appeared to him had said to him other things, which he must never, so long as he should live, reveal to any man. And it is to be believed that these discourses were secret things spoken to him by that sacred Seraph, who so marvelously appeared to him on the Cross, and which, perhaps, it was not lawful to utter to men. When the lover of Christ had been transformed by his true love into his own image, having fulfilled the forty days which he had thus spent in solitude before the feast of the Archangel Michael, this angelical man, Francis, descended from the mount, bearing with him the image of the Crucified, engraven, not on tables of wood nor stone by the hand of the artificer, but written on his members of flesh by the finger of the living God. And because it is written that it is good *to conceal the secret of the king,* therefore this man, who was conscious of so royal a secret, endeavored to conceal its sacred signs from the eyes of all men. But inasmuch as God is wont for His own glory to reveal the great things which He works, the Lord Himself, who had secretly impressed these tokens, openly manifested many miracles by their power, that the hidden and miraculous virtue of these Stigmata might be clearly made known by many signs.

In the country of Rieti, a grievous pestilence broke out, which cruelly consumed both sheep and cattle, and for which no remedy could be found. But a certain man who feared God was warned by a vision at night, that he should go with all speed to the hermitage of the friars, and ask for the water in which Francis, the servant of God, who then abode there, had washed his hands and feet, and that he should sprinkle this water upon the animals. He arose, therefore, in the morning and came to the place, and having secretly obtained some of this water from the companions of the holy man, he sprinkled it over the diseased cattle and sheep. Marvellous to relate, no sooner had a drop of this water touched the sick animals, as they lay on the ground, than they immediately recovered their strength, and, as if they had felt no sickness, they hastened to pasture.

Around the aforesaid mountain of Alvernia, before the holy man dwelt there, by reason of the clouds which arose from the mountain, a violent tempest of destructive hail was accustomed to destroy all the fruit; but after that blessed apparition the hail ceased, to the great amazement of the inhabitants of the place, the unwonted serenity of the sky thus manifesting the excellence of that celestial vision in which the Stigmata were impressed.

Once, on a winter's day, by reason of the weakness of his body and the steep and difficult path, he was riding upon an ass belonging to a poor man, and was compelled to take shelter for the night under a rock, to avoid the snow which had fallen and was falling heavily in those parts. For, being delayed by these impediments, he could not reach the place of his destination. Now, the Saint, hearing that the poor man to whom the ass belonged was lamenting himself bitterly and trembling with cold, changing now to one place, now to another, because, being lightly and poorly clothed, he could find no relief from the bitter cold, Francis, all on fire with divine love, stretched forth his hand and touched him, when, marvellous to say, the touch of that sacred hand which had received the fire of the seraphical sign banished all sense of cold, so that the poor man waxed warm both within and without, as if he had felt the power of a burning fiery furnace; so that, being comforted in body and mind, he lay down to rest, and slept sweetly amid the rocks and snow, as he himself afterwards affirmed. Certain it is, therefore, by all these tokens, that these Sacred Stigmata were impressed by the power of Him Who, by the agency of the Seraph, purified, illuminated, and inflamed; inasmuch as the said Stigmata, purifying the air without from pestilence, delivered and healed the beasts, and with marvellous efficacy calmed the tempest and warmed frozen bodies, as came to pass also after his death, which we shall hereafter notice. Therefore, although he sought with diligent care to conceal the treasure which he had found in the field, yet it could not be hid, nor could he prevent the Stigmata in his hands and feet from being seen, although he kept his hands almost always covered, and from that time forward always wore shoes on his feet. During his lifetime many of his brethren saw these Stigmata clearly, who, although for their great sanctity they were men worthy of all credit, yet to remove all doubt they affirmed what they had seen on oath. Several of the cardinals, who lived with great familiarity with the holy man, saw them also, and composed hymns and antiphons in honor of the Sacred Stigmata, thus by their words as well as by their writings giving testimony to this truth. The Supreme Pontiff, Alexander, also, when preaching to the people, in the presence of many of the friars, of whom I was one, affirmed that, in the lifetime of the Saint, he had seen the Sacred

Stigmata with his own eyes. At his death they were seen by more than fifty brethren together, and also by Clare, that virgin most devoted to God, with many of her Sisters and an innumerable company of seculars, who, as will be seen hereafter, kissed them with great devotion and touched them with her hands, to ascertain the truth of the miracle, and the wound in the side also, which during his lifetime he concealed so carefully that no one ever saw or could see it, except by stealth. A brother who ministered to him with great care once induced him, with pious craft, to take off his tunic, that he might brush it, and then, looking attentively, he saw the wound, which he contrived hastily to touch with his three fingers, and thus ascertained its figure and size, not only by sight, but also by touch. By the same artifice another friar, who was his Vicar at the time, also saw it. Another friar, of great simplicity, who was his companion, was once rubbing his shoulders to relieve a pain which he suffered there, and accidentally touched the sacred wound, thereby causing him exceeding pain. From that time forward he wore his inner garment in such wise as to conceal the wound in the side. But the brothers who washed it, and from time to time brushed his tunic, found them stained with blood, and thus came to know with positive certainty the existence of the sacred wound, which after his death they plainly saw, contemplating and venerating it with many other witnesses.

Go forth, therefore, O valiant servant of Christ, for thus bearing the arms and insignia of thine invincible Leader Himself, thou shalt overcome every adversary. Bear the standard of the Most High King, the sight of which animates every warrior of the divine army. Bear the seal of the Supreme Pontiff, Christ, stamped undeniably and authentically upon all thy words and deeds, so that they may be accepted duly by all men; and even because of this Stigmata of the Lord Jesus which thou bearest in thy body, let no man dare to trouble thee, but rather let every servant of Christ bear thee tender and devoted affection. For by these most certain signs, not by two or three witnesses only, but by a superabundance of proofs, that seal is made plain to all men (God having made it visible in thee and by thee, so as to take away every veil or shadow of excuse), that they may believe and be established in faith, and by faith may be raised to hope and enkindled with charity. For now is truly fulfilled that first vision of thine, viz., that, being chosen by the mercy of Christ to be His captain, thou wast to be armed with celestial weapons, and signed with the sign of the Cross. Now, the vision which thou didst behold in the beginning of thy conversion, that vision of the Crucified which pierced thee as with a sword of compassion, and the voice which thou heardest from the Cross as from the high throne and secret mercy-seat of Christ, bidding thee be conformed to the image of the Crucified, are shown to be undoubted truths. Now may it be surely and firmly believed that what Sylvester beheld soon after thy conversion was no fantastical imagination, but a celestial revelation, for he beheld a Cross marvelously issuing from thy mouth; and the holy Br. Pacificus also beheld two blades crossing thy body in the form of a Cross; and, moreover (as has been said before), that angelic man, Monardos, when St. Anthony was preaching on the title of the Cross, beheld thee raised in the air in the form of the Cross. Again, that which was shown to thee near the end of thy life, even the similitude of that lofty Seraph bearing the humble image of the Crucified which enkindled thee within and signed thee without, shows thee to be, as it were, another angel descending from the East, and having the sign of the living God. This, I say, gives strength and credibility to all the things before said, and receives from them a testimony to its truth. For behold these six apparitions of the Cross of Christ, thus marvelously shown according to the order of divers times, in thee and concerning thee, are, as it were, six steps to the seventh, to which thou hast now attained, and where thou dost now repose. For the Cross of Christ, which at the beginning of thy conversion was proposed to thee, which was received by thee, and ever throughout the whole course of thy life was faithfully carried by thee, both in thine own person and as an example to others, has proved to the clearest demonstration that thou hast attained to the summit of evangelical perfection, so that no truly devout man can deny the wisdom of Christ, shown forth in thy body of dust, and no truly faithful man may deny, no truly humble man may despise, that which has been impressed upon thee by the divine power as most worthy to be received and accepted by all men.

Chapter XIV

RANCIS, being thus crucified with Christ, both in the flesh and in the spirit, not only burned with seraphic love towards God, but thirsted with Christ crucified for the salvation of a multitude of souls. Now, it came to pass, as he could not walk on foot because of the nails which were in his feet, he was obliged to be carried through the cities and other places whither he wished to go, that he might thus encourage others to carry the Cross of Christ. For he was wont to say to his brethren: "Let us begin, at last, my brethren, to serve the Lord our God, for hitherto we have done but little." He burned also with an ardent desire to return to the first steps of his humility, that, as at the beginning, he might serve the lepers, and excite his weak body, now broken by continual labors, to its former toils. And he proposed, by the help and guidance of Christ, to do great things; and while his members seemed weary and feeble, being strong and fervent in spirit, he hoped to wage a fresh warfare against the enemy, and to attain a glorious triumph. For there is no place for languor or sloth where the stimulus of love is ever urging to greater things. And such was the harmony between his spirit and his flesh, and such the obedience of the flesh to the spirit, that in his efforts to obtain perfect and complete sanctity, the flesh not only made no resistance to the spirit, but even aided and prevented it. Now that the holy man might increase his chain of merits, which are ever

119

made perfect by patience, he began to suffer from so many infirmities, that there was scarcely one of his members but was tormented by immense pain and suffering. At last, by reason of these various long and continued infirmities, his flesh was consumed, and there remained but the skin attached to his bones. Yet, although his body was thus afflicted with grievous torments, he never called them by the name of pains, but spoke of them as *his sisters*. Once being more grievously tormented than usual, a certain simple brother said to him: "Brother, pray to God that He would deal more gently with thee, for it seems to me that His hand is heavier upon thee than is meet." Which, when the holy man heard, he cried with great abhorrence: "But that I know the purity of thy simplicity, I should from henceforth abhor thy company, for that thou hast dared to find fault with the divine judgments which are executed upon me." And although he was all broken by the long endurance of his sufferings, he cast himself upon the ground, all his weak bones being shattered by the fall. And kissing the ground, he said: "I thank Thee, O Lord, my God, for these my pains, and I beseech Thee, O Lord, to increase them a hundredfold, for this shall be most acceptable to me, that Thou spare not to afflict me with suffering, because the fulfillment of Thy Holy Will is to me an overflowing consolation." He seemed to the brethren like another Job, the fortitude of his mind increasing with the suffering of his body. A long time beforehand he predicted the day of his death, and when the time of that transit drew near, he said to the brethren that he must shortly lay aside the tabernacle of his body, as it had been revealed to him by Christ. Two years, then, after the impression of the Sacred Stigmata, that is, in the twentieth year after his conversion, he was attacked by many infirmities; and as a rock struck and tried by many blows, or as a true stone, which was to be built into the edifice of the heavenly Jerusalem, or as some fair work which, by the force of the hammer of many tribulations, was to be brought to a perfect form, he ordered the brethren to carry him to St. Mary of the Portiuncula, that where he had received the spirit of grace he might give up the spirit of life. Having, therefore, been brought thither, and desiring to give a true proof to all men that he had no longer anything in common with the world in that grievous and painful sickness, he laid aside his habit, and laid himself prostrate on the bare earth, that in the last hour in which the enemy would attack him with all his fury he might wrestle naked with his naked adversary. Lying thus on the earth, with his face raised according to his custom to Heaven, and intent upon its glory, with his left hand he covered the wound on his right side, and said to his brethren: "I have done my part; may Christ teach you to do yours!" And all his holy companions wept, for they were filled with great compassion. One among them, whom the man of God called his *guardian,* knowing his wish by divine inspiration, arose and brought a tunic and a cord, and offering them to the poor man of Christ, he said: "I bring thee these as to one who has made himself poor for the love of God; receive them by the command of holy obedience." Then did the holy man rejoice with great gladness of heart, when he saw that he had kept faith with his lady, poverty, even to the end; and raising his hands to Heaven, he gave thanks to Christ, his Lord, that, being delivered from every burden, he was free to go to Him. And all these things he did out of his zeal for poverty, so that he would not have even a habit but what was lent him by another. For in all things, assuredly, he desired to be conformed to Christ crucified, Who hung naked upon the Cross, in poverty and pain. And therefore, as at the beginning of his conversion, he cast off his garment before the Bishop, so at the end of his life he desired to depart naked out of this world. And he commanded the brethren who were around him, in virtue of charity and obedience, that when they should perceive that he was dead, they would leave him thus upon the ground for so long a space of time as it would take a man to walk gently for a mile. Oh! Most truly Christian man, conformed living to the life of Christ, and dying to the dying of Christ, studying in death to be perfectly conformed to the death of Christ, and found worthy to be adorned with His express similitude!

The hour of his departure being at hand, he commanded all the brethren who were in that place to be called to him, and comforted them with consoling words concerning his death, exhorting them with fatherly affection to the divine love. He spoke to them at length concerning patience, poverty, and faithful obedience to the Holy Roman Church, preferring the Holy Gospel to all other laws and institutions. And as all the brethren surrounded him, he extended his hands over them in the form of a cross, crossing his arms in the form of that sign which he had ever loved; and so he blessed all the brethren, whether present or absent, in the Name and in the power of the Crucified. Then he added: "Farewell, my children, abide in the fear of the Lord, and ever persevere therein. And when any temptation or trouble approaches you say: *Blessed are they who persevere in those things which they have begun.* And now I go to God, to Whose grace I commend you all."

When he had finished these loving admonitions, this man, most dear to God, commanded that the Book of the Gospels should be brought to him, and that the place of the Gospel of St. John should be read to him which begins with these words: *Ante diem festum paschae.* And then, as best he could, he broke forth into that verse of the psalm, *Voce mea ad Dominum clamavi, voce mea ad Dominum deprecatus sum,* and so continued repeating the psalm until he came to the verse, *Me exspectant justi, donec retribuas mihi.* All these mysteries being then accomplished in him, his most holy soul being set free and absorbed in the abyss of the divine glory, the blessed man slept in the Lord. One of his brethren and disciples saw that blessed soul under the appearance of a glorious star, borne upwards by a white cloud, and so carried as upon many waters, straight to Heaven; and that glorious cloud betokened the sublime purity of sanctity and the fulness of heavenly wisdom and abundant grace, by which the holy man had merited an entrance into that palace of light and peace, where for all eternity he reposes in Christ.

At that time Br. Augustine, a holy and just man, was minister of the Friars at Lavoro: he being at the point of death, and having for a long time lost the use of speech, exclaimed suddenly, in the hearing of all who stood around: "Wait for me, Father, wait for me; I am coming with thee." When the Friars, in great amazement, asked him to whom he thus spoke, he replied promptly, "See you not our Father Francis, who is going up to Heaven?" And having said this, his soul immediately departed from his body, and he followed his most holy Father.

At the same time the Bishop of Assisi was making a devout pilgrimage to the church of St. Michael, on Mount Gargano. To him the Blessed Francis appeared on the very night of his departure, saying: "Behold, I leave the world and go to Heaven." When the Bishop arose in the morning he related to his companions what he had seen, and having made strict inquiry on his return to Assisi, he discovered certainly that, at the very hour revealed to him by the vision, the Blessed

Father had departed from this world.

Certain birds which love the light, and have a great horror of darkness, at the hour of the holy man's transit from earth, which was the time at which twilight is wont to set in, came in great multitudes over the roof of the house, and flew round and round it joyfully for a long time together, giving clear and joyous testimony to the glory of the Saint who had been wont to invite them to sing the praises of God.

Chapter XV

HUS Francis, the servant and friend of the Most High, the founder and leader of the Friars Minor, the professor of poverty, the model of penance, the preacher of truth, the mirror of sanctity, the example of all evangelical perfection, being prevented by grace from on high, ascended from the base to the summit of perfection.

This marvellous man, whom God glorified in his mortal life, turning his poverty to exceeding great riches, exalting his humility, turning his mortification to life, his simplicity to prudence, making him conspicuous for all good works, having been made glorious in life by the power of the Lord, became beyond comparison more glorious in death. For when the holy man had departed from this life, and his sacred spirit had entered its eternal house, there to drink abundantly from the fountain of glory, certain wonderful tokens of its future glory were left on his body, that the most sacred flesh which, having been crucified with sin, had already passed into a new creature, and, by a singular privilege, bore the image of Christ, might by a new miracle show forth the glory of the resurrection. For now were discerned in those blessed members the nails which, by the divine power, had been marvelously fashioned out of his own flesh, so that, being pressed on either side, they moved to the other. In his body was found also an open wound in the side, made by no human hand, like to the wound which our

Redeemer bore for us, and from which issued forth the sacraments of redemption and regeneration. The appearance of the nails was black like iron; the wound in his side was red and rounded, after the appearance of a beautiful rose. All the rest of his body, which had been dark by nature, and became darker by reason of his infirmities, was now of a marvellous whiteness, and so dazzling as to show forth the brightness of the second state of glory. His limbs seemed to those who touched them so soft and supple as to appear like the limbs of a young child, thus figuring the innocence with which he was adorned. Now, beholding the black nails in that white flesh, and the wound in the side ruddy as a rose in spring, it is no marvel that all who saw them were filled with wonder and admiration. The sons wept for the loss of so beloved a father, and yet were filled with unspeakable gladness when they kissed the seals of the King of Heaven; the novelty of the miracle changed their tears into joy, and the understanding remained in amazement at the sight. So unwonted and wonderful a sight was, to all who beheld it, a confirmation of faith, and an incitement to love to those who heard of it; it afforded matter of admiration, and excited a desire to behold it. As soon, therefore, as the departure of the holy Father was heard of, and the fame of the miracle was spread abroad, all the people ran together to see with their own eyes what might remove every doubt from their minds, and satisfy the love of their hearts. Many of the citizens of Assisi were admitted to see and kiss the Sacred Stigmata. Among these was a certain soldier, a learned and prudent man, named Jerome, held in high estimation in the city, who, doubting of the Sacred Stigmata, and being incredulous like another Thomas, more boldly and eagerly than the rest moved the nails in the presence of his fellow-citizens, and touched with his own hands the hands and feet of the holy man; and while he thus touched these palpable signs of the wounds of Christ, his heart was healed and freed from every wound of doubt. And he having thus received such certain knowledge of the truth, became a most effectual witness of the same, and confirmed it by oath on the Holy Gospels.

Now, all the brethren and children of the holy Father who had been called to witness his departure, with the great multitude of people who were come together on the night in which Christ's glorious confessor departed to Him, passed the night in the praises of God, so that it seemed not to be the requiem for the departed, but the rejoicing of angels. When the morning dawned, the whole multitude took branches of trees, and with many tapers and torches, and with hymns and canticles, they bore the sacred body to the city of Assisi. And passing by the church of St. Damian, where that noble virgin, Clare, now glorious in Heaven, abode with the virgins her sisters, the holy body, adorned with celestial jewels, remained there awhile, till those holy virgins could see and kiss them. Then with great joy they came to the city, and laid the precious treasure which they had brought with them with all reverence in the church of St. George. For in that place, when he was yet a child, he had learnt the first beginning of letters; there he had begun to preach; and lastly, in that same spot he found his first resting-place.

The venerable Father passed away from the wreck of this world in the year of our Lord's Incarnation, 1226, on the 4th of October, on the evening of Saturday, and he was buried on Sunday. The sacred and blessed body, glorified by divine grace, began at once to work manifold and great miracles, that the excellence of his sanctity, which during his life in the flesh had been made known to the world by the example of true and perfect justice, whereby he had directed and reformed the manners of men, now that he was reigning with Christ, was proved by the miracles wrought by the divine power in confirmation of the faith by which he was believed to be in Heaven.

These glorious miracles, having become known in divers parts of the world, and the great benefits attained by his merits having excited great multitudes of men to greater devotion to our Lord Jesus Christ, and deeper reverence for His Saint, the sound both of these words and works came to the ears of the Sovereign Pontiff, Gregory IX. The Holy Pontiff, knowing his marvellous sanctity by certain and undoubted testimony, not only of the miracles wrought by him since his death, but also by his own manifold experience of his holy life when he saw and conversed with him on earth, doubted not that he had been glorified by the Lord in Heaven. To cooperate, therefore, with Christ, Whose Vicar he was, he determined with pious counsel and holy consideration to pay to the holy man that veneration and honor of which he knew him to be most worthy. And in order to add greater certainty to the glorification of this most holy man, he caused all the miracles wrought by him and related by others to be examined by those members of the College of Cardinals who were least favorable to the undertaking. These having diligently investigated and approved all the matters laid before them, he determined, with the consent of all the cardinals and prelates then present, to proceed to the canonization; and coming himself in person to the city of Assisi in the year of our Lord's Incarnation, 1228, on Sunday, the 6th of July, with many ceremonies and great solemnity, which it would be too long here to narrate, he inscribed the Blessed Father in the catalogue of the Saints.

In the year of our Lord 1230, all the Friars of the

Order being assembled in general chapter at Assisi, that body, consecrated to the Lord, was transferred to the church erected to his honor on the 21st of May. While the sacred treasure, signed with the signet of the Most High King, was being carried from one place to another, he, whose effigy was impressed upon it, was pleased that, by its health-giving ardor, the affections of many of the faithful should he drawn to follow after Christ; and most worthy was this of him who while in life was so dear to God, who by the grace of contemplation had been transported like Enoch into Paradise, and by the zeal of his charity had been carried like Elias to Heaven in a chariot of fire. Even his blessed bones, which, having been transplanted from this barren earth, began to flourish among the heavenly flowers of the celestial garden, gave forth a sweet and marvellous odor of sanctity, from the place where they were found; and certain it is that as, when he was in life, this blessed man was illustrious and renowned by many marvellous tokens of virtue and sanctity, so, from the day of his death to the present hour, he has been glorified in divers parts of the world by manifold prodigies and miracles; so that, through the divine power, by his merits help is afforded to the blind, the deaf, the dumb, the lame, the dropsical, the paralytic, the possessed, the lepers, and to those who are tempest-tossed or languish in captivity. He relieves all infirmities, necessities, and perils. Nay, by the marvellous resurrection of many from the dead is made known to the faithful the power of his merits, and the glorious might of the Most High, Who is marvellous in His saints, to Whom be honor and glory forever and ever. Amen.

Of Certain Miracles Wrought
After His Death

First: By the power of the Sacred Stigmata

O the honor of Almighty God, and to the glory of our Blessed Father Francis, we will now relate, on the authority of approved writings, certain miracles wrought by him after his glorification in Heaven. And we have thought well to begin with those in which the mystery of the Cross of Jesus was shown forth and its glory renewed. For the new man, Francis, manifested his renewal when, by a singular privilege never before granted to anyone, the Sacred Stigmata were impressed upon his flesh, and he appeared adorned with those glorious signs, being conformed in the body of this death to the Body of the Crucified. Whereof, if any human tongue should attempt to speak, it would fail to praise it worthily. For, assuredly, all the thoughts of that man of God, whether in public or in private, were devoted to the Cross of the Lord. And in order that the sign of that holy Cross, impressed on his heart in the very beginning of his conversion, should also mark his body exteriorly, being wholly devoted thereto, he took the habit of penance, bearing thus outwardly the image of the Cross, that, as his spirit within was clothed with his crucified Lord, so should his body also be invested with the armor of the Cross, that so his army should fight for the Lord under the same sign by which God Himself overcame all the powers of the air. But from the beginning of that time when he began the warfare of the Cross, many of its mysteries began to manifest themselves around him, as will plainly appear to anyone who deeply considers the whole course of his life, where it is seen by the sevenfold apparition of the Cross of the Lord, that he was transformed by an exceeding and ecstatic love, in every thought, act and affection, into the image of the Crucified. Meet, therefore, it was, that the clemency of the Supreme and Eternal King of Heaven, Who condescends beyond all human belief to those who love Him, should impress upon him the outward insignia of His Cross, which he already bore in his body, that he who exceeded all other men in his marvellous love of the Cross should be made also a marvellous testimony of the glory of the Cross. For the undeniable confirmation of this stupendous miracle, we have not only the testimony of witnesses in every way credible, who had palpable and visible evidence thereof, but it has been attested also by wonderful visions and miracles which occurred after his death, and which are sufficient to banish every shadow of doubt from the minds of men. As a proof of this, Pope Gregory IX (to whom the holy man had foretold, long before it came to pass, that he should be raised to the chair of the Apostle), before he inscribed in the catalogue of the Saints this standard-bearer of the Cross, felt some doubt and hesitation of mind with regard to the wound in the side. On a certain night, then, as the Pontiff was afterwards wont to relate with many tears, the Blessed Francis appeared to him in a dream, and with an unwonted severity in his countenance, reproving him for the doubt which lurked in his heart, raised his right arm, discovered the wound, and commanded that a vessel should be brought to receive the blood which issued from his side. The Supreme Pontiff, still in vision, brought him the vessel, which seemed to be filled even to the brim with the blood which flowed from his side. From that day forward he felt such great devotion and fervent zeal for the honor of that miracle, that he could never endure to hear any doubt, or denial, or proud contradiction of the truth of those glorious Stigmata, but severely reproved anyone who ventured thus to speak.

A certain Friar of the Order of St. Francis, who bore the office of a preacher, and had a great reputation for virtue, at first believed firmly in the truth of these Sacred Stigmata. But afterwards he desired (out of a feeling of human pride) to inquire concerning the grounds of this miracle, and he began to be troubled by a certain doubtful scruple concerning it. And this doubt gaining ground upon him, he continued for many days together to sustain a great conflict within himself. To this Friar, as he was sleeping one night, the Blessed Francis appeared, with his feet all covered with mire, and with a certain humble severity and patient displeasure on his countenance. "And what," said he, "are these conflicts and vile doubts within thee? Behold my hands and my feet." Then the Friar saw the pierced hands, but the Stigmata in the feet he could not see, because of the mire which covered them. "Remove," said the Saint, "the mire from my feet, and you shall see the place of the nails." Then he devoutly took hold of the feet, and it seemed that, as he washed away the mire, he touched the place of the nails with his hands. And when he awoke his face was bathed with tears, and thus, with abundance of weeping and a public confession, he endeavored to cleanse those first thoughts and affections, which he now saw to be evil and defiled.

There was a certain matron in the city of Rome, noble both in birth and life, who had chosen St. Francis for her advocate, and had his picture in a private oratory, where she prayed to her Father in secret. One day, when she was in prayer, and gazing on the picture of the Saint, she saw that it had not the Sacred Stigmata, at which she began greatly to wonder and to grieve. Yet it was no marvel that the picture had not what was omitted by the painter. Having anxiously considered for many days what was the cause of this omission, she suddenly beheld those wonderful signs appear in the picture, as they are ordinarily depicted. In great astonishment, she called trembling to one of her daughters, whom she had devoted to God, and asked her whether she remembered that this picture had hitherto been without the Stigmata. The daughter affirmed it, and declared upon oath that it had been until now without the Sacred Stigmata, and that she now saw them there for the first time. But because the human mind, often by its own heaviness, helps us to fall, and makes that which is true to seem doubtful, an injurious doubt immediately entered the heart of the lady, and she thought that perhaps the Stigmata had been thus painted from the beginning. But lest the first miracle should be despised, the power of God now added a second, for the Stigmata mediately disappeared, leaving the portrait devoid of them, so that the second miracle was a proof of the first.

It happened in the city of Ilerda, in Catalonia, that a good man, named John, who was very devout to St. Francis, had to pass through a street, in which certain men were lying in wait to kill him, not for any enmity that they bore him, but because of his likeness to another whom they hated, and who was then in his company. One of them sprang forth from the ambush, and believing him to be his enemy, wounded him with so many dagger-strokes as to leave him without hope of life. For the first stroke had almost cut off his shoulder and one of his arms, and another inflicted such a wound on his breast that the blood which issued from it extinguished six candles all burning together. The poor man's cure was considered impossible by all the physicians, for the wounds began to putrefy, and gave forth such an intolerable odor that his own wife could scarcely endure it. All human remedies being hopeless, the good man had recourse to the Blessed Father St. Francis, and that with the greater devotion because, at the moment when he was wounded, he had invoked his protection and that of the blessed virgin Clare. And, behold, as the sufferer lay alone on his bed, frequently calling on the name of Francis, and repeating it with many cries, one stood by him in the habit of a Friar Minor, who, as it seemed to him, came in by a window, and calling him by his name, said, "Because thou hast trusted in me, behold, the Lord will deliver thee." And when the sick man asked him who he was, he answered, "I am Francis." And immediately drawing near to him, he loosened all the bandages and ligatures from his wounds, and seemed to anoint them with ointment. No sooner did the poor man feel the sweet touch of those sacred hands, which, by the power of the Saviour's Stigmata, had the virtue of healing, than all the corruption departed from the wounds, and the flesh was restored, so that at the same time the wounds were closed, and the sick man restored to perfect health. And when this was done the Blessed Father departed. The wounded man, feeling himself made whole, immediately began to praise God with great joy, and to thank the Blessed Francis. He then called his wife, who came with all haste, and seeing him standing upon his feet whom she verily thought to have buried on the morrow, being filled with incredible amazement, she roused the whole neighborhood with her cries. Her friends came running together, and believing the wounded man to be delirious, endeavored to force him to return to his bed; but he resisted them, affirming and showing that he was perfectly cured, insomuch that all who beheld him were astonished, and could scarcely believe but what they saw was a dream and a phantom; he whom they had beheld covered with frightful wounds, already putrefying and corrupt, now standing before them full of health and gladness. Then he who had been made whole spoke thus to them: "Fear not, nor disbelieve that which you see with your own eyes; for St. Francis has but just now departed; he touched me with his sacred hands and perfectly healed my wounds." Now, the fame of this miracle being spread abroad, all men were filled with wonder and gladness; and with loud praises they extolled Francis, the standard-bearer of Christ. And fitting it was that our Blessed Father St. Francis, being dead according to the flesh, and alive with Christ, by the wonderful manifestation of his presence and the sweet touch of his sacred hands, should restore health to that man wounded even to death, seeing that he also bore in his own body His Stigmata Who, by His merciful death and marvellous resurrection, healed, by the virtue of His wounds, the whole human race which had been wounded and left half dead.

In Potenza, a city of Apulia, there lived a certain clerk, named Roger, an honorable man and a Canon of the Cathedral Church. He having been long suffering under a severe sickness, went into that church to pray, where was a picture of the Blessed Francis, representing the glorious Stigmata. As he looked upon it, he began to doubt concerning that sublime miracle, as if it were something strange and impossible. As he was inwardly wounded by these idle thoughts, he felt himself severely wounded in his left hand under his glove, and at the same time heard a noise, like the whizzing of an arrow from a bow. He immediately took off his glove, desiring to see with his eyes what had already been impressed upon the senses of touch and hearing. His hand having been previously unwounded, he now saw in the midst of the palm a wound which seemed to proceed from an arrow-stroke, and so intense was the burning pain, that he felt as if he must faint. Marvellous to say, there was no vestige of a hole in the glove, so that the secrecy of the wound in the heart corresponded with the secrecy of the wound inflicted as his penalty. For two whole days together he cried out with the intensity of the pain, and confessed to all around him the incredulity which had lurked in his heart. And he confessed and solemnly professed his belief in the Sacred Stigmata of St. Francis, every shadow of doubt having departed from him. And thus he suppliantly besought the Saint of God to help him by virtue of his Sacred Stigmata, pouring forth many heartfelt prayers, mingled with torrents of tears. Wonderful to say, having cast away his incredulity, the healing of his body followed that of his mind. All the pain vanished, the burning was cooled, no vestige of the wound remained; and so it was that, by the clemency and providence of God, the hidden sickness of the mind was cured by the visible cautery of the flesh, and as soon as the mind was healed the flesh also was made whole. That man became most humble and devout to God, and a loving and faithful servant to the Order of Friars Minor. This wonderful miracle was affirmed by many upon oath, and authenticated by the Bishop's seal, so that the knowledge of it has come down to us.

There is, therefore, no room for doubt concerning the Sacred Stigmata; neither, because God is good, should the eye of any man be evil with regard to this thing, as if it befitted not the Eternal Goodness to bestow such gifts upon men. For if, by that seraphical love, many members came to be united to Christ, their Head, so that, arrayed in that armor, they might show themselves worthy of Him and of His gifts, and thereafter be exalted to a like glory with Him in Heaven, there is no man of sound mind but must see that this redounds to the glory of Christ alone.

Of many Dead who were Raised to Life.

 N Mount Marcano, a place near Benevento, a certain woman, who had a special devotion to St. Francis, went the way of all flesh. Now, all the clergy of that place being assembled round the corpse to keep the accustomed vigils, and say the usual psalms and prayers, suddenly that woman rose on her feet, in presence of them all, on the bier where she lay, and calling to her one of the priests present, who was her godfather: "Father," she said, "I wish to confess. As soon as I was dead, I was to be sent to a dreadful dungeon, because I had never confessed a certain sin which I will now make known to thee. But St. Francis, whom I had ever devoutly served, having prayed for me, I have been suffered to return to the body, that, having revealed that sin, I may be made worthy of eternal life. And here, before your eyes, as soon as I shall have disclosed it, I shall depart to my promised rest." She made her confession, therefore, trembling, to the priest, and having received absolution, quietly lay down on the bier, and slept peacefully in the Lord.

At Parmaco, in Apulia, there was a maiden of tender age, the most beloved child of her father and mother, who was brought to death by a grievous sickness; her parents having no longer any hope of succession, accounted themselves to be dead in her death. All their relations and friends came together, weeping, to that sorrowful burial; the unhappy mother lay so overwhelmed with unspeakable grief and sadness, that she took no heed of anything which passed around her.

Meanwhile St. Francis, accompanied by a single Friar, vouchsafed to appear to her, and consoled the desolate woman, who was very devout to him, with compassionate words, saying: "Weep no more; for the quenched light of thy candlestick, for which now thou weepest, is restored to thee by my intercession." At these words the woman immediately arose, and declaring to all what the Saint had said to her, she forbade them to bury the corpse, but calling upon St. Francis with lively faith, she took her dead daughter's hand, and raised her up alive and well, in the presence of all who stood wondering round her.

The Friars at Nocera once asked a man, named Peter, to lend them his cart, of which they stood in need; but he answered them with abuse instead of giving them the help they needed, and in answer to the alms asked in honor of St. Francis, he blasphemed his holy name. But he soon repented of his folly, being struck with a divine fear lest the vengeance of God should fall upon him, as speedily came to pass. For his only son fell sick at that time, and not long afterwards died. The miserable father cast himself on the ground, and ceased not to call, with many tears, upon Francis, the Saint of God, crying: "It is I who have sinned, I who have spoken wickedly; punish me, therefore, in my own person. Oh, Saint of God! restore to me, now penitent, him whom thou hast taken from me, because I blasphemed thee. I restore and give myself wholly to thee, and devote myself forever to thy service, for I will continually offer to Christ, for the glory of thy name, a devout sacrifice of praise." At these words, wonderful to relate, the boy arose, and forbade his father to weep, saying that, having been already dead, by the intercession of the Blessed Francis he had been restored to life.

There was a boy, hardly seven years old, the son of

a notary at Rome, who, desiring to follow his mother when she was going to the church of St. Mark, was compelled by her to remain at home; in his boyish eagerness he threw himself out of a window into the street, and was killed on the spot by the fall. The mother, who was not yet far from the house, heard the noise of the fall, and fearing for the safety of her beloved child, returned in all haste; finding that he had been thus suddenly and miserably taken from her, she began to strike herself with her own hands, and with mournful cries excited all the neighbors to lament with her. A certain Friar Minor, named Ralph, who had come thither to preach, then drew near to the child, and being full of faith spoke thus to the father: "Believest thou that Francis, the Saint of God, is able to raise thy son from the dead by the love which he ever bore to Christ, Who was crucified to restore life to men?" The father replied that he firmly believed it, and faithfully promised to devote himself forever to the service of that Saint of God, if, by his merits, he should be found worthy to receive so great a favor. Then the Friar, together with his companion, prostrated himself in prayer, exhorting and encouraging all present to pray also. When they had thus prayed, the child began to open his eyes and raise his arms; then he rose upon his feet in the presence of them all, and being well and strong, he began to walk, having been restored by the marvellous power of the Saint both to life and health.

In the city of Capua, a little boy was playing upon the banks of the river with many others, and unexpectedly falling into the water, was carried away by the force of the torrent, and buried beneath the sand. At the cries of all the other children, who were playing with him on the bank, a great multitude of people quickly assembled together. Then they began to cry, and suppliantly and devoutly to invoke the merits of the Blessed Francis, praying him to have regard to the faith of the child's parents, who were very devout to him, and to deliver their son from death. A certain man who was known to be a good swimmer, hearing from afar these cries, which rose to Heaven, searched the river to find the child's body, and at last, calling upon the name and help of St. Francis, came to a place where the sand had formed a kind of sepulchre round the body of the dead child, whom he drew forth and carried out of the water, grieving much to see that he was dead. Then all the people gathered round to see the dead child, weeping and crying, "Oh, St. Francis, restore the child to his father." Then suddenly the boy, to the joy and wonder of all, arose alive and well, and begged to be taken to the church of St. Francis, that he might devoutly return thanks to him by whose power he knew that he had been miraculously restored to life.

In the city of Sepa, in a place called Colonna, a house suddenly fell upon a poor young man and killed him. Many men and women ran together from every part at the noise of the fall, and having cleared away the stones and wood, they at last found the unhappy youth dead, and brought him to his sorrowful mother, who broke forth into bitter tears and exclaimed, "Oh, St. Francis, St. Francis, give me back my child!" and not she alone, but all who were present, besought the aid of the blessed Saint. But finding the young man still without speech or sense, they laid him upon a bier, intending to bury him on the following day. The mother, nevertheless, having great faith in the Lord by the merit of His Saint, made a vow to cover the altar of St. Francis with a new pall if he would restore her son to life. And behold, about midnight, the boy began to revive, his limbs recovered their heat; and being alive, well, and strong, he began to give thanks and praises to God and to the Blessed Francis, calling upon the clergy and the people who came together to join with him in praise and thanksgiving.

There was another young man, called Geraldino, of Ragusa, who, in the time of the vintage, as he came out of the vineyard, went to fill the vessels of wine from the great tun which was under the winepress, when some great stones, which were suddenly loosened, fell upon his head and crushed it, wounding him to death. The father, having heard the noise, ran to the place, and despairing of the safety of his son, approached no nearer to him, but left him as he found him, under the stones. The other vintagers, running together in all haste when they heard the feeble cry of the son, were filled, like the father, with great sorrow, and drew the young man, already dead, from beneath the ruin. But the father, prostrate at the feet of Jesus Christ, humbly besought Him, by the merits of St. Francis, to vouchsafe to restore to him his only son; and uttering prayer upon prayer, he promised to perform many works of charity, and to visit the sepulchre of the holy man, together with his son, if he would raise him from the dead. Suddenly the young man, whose body was all broken and crushed, being restored to life and perfect health, arose full of joy in the presence of them all, and reproving those who were weeping over him, affirmed that by the prayers of St. Francis he had been restored to life.

The Saint raised also another dead man in Germany, whereof the Blessed Father, Pope Gregory, certified the Friars of the Order, and congratulated them greatly by his apostolical letters at the time of the translation of the body of the Saint, when they came together to that translation, and to the general Chapter. The manner of that miracle I do not relate, because, in truth, I know it not, believing the testimony of the Holy Father to be more worthy of credit than any other affirmation that could be made.

Of many whom he Delivered from the Danger of Death.

N the neighborhood of the city of Rome there was a certain nobleman, named Ridolpho, whose wife was very devout to God, and he often received the Friars Minor, not only from the virtue of hospitality, but out of reverence and love for the Blessed Francis. It happened one night that the warder of the castle, who watched on its highest tower, had laid down to rest upon a heap of wood, which, becoming loose, began to fall, and thus the poor man fell with it, first upon the palace roof, and thence to the ground. The noise of the fall awakened the whole family, and at the news of the warder's accident, the lord of the castle, with his lady and the Friars, came in haste to the spot; but he who had fallen from so great a height was in so deep a sleep that he was not awakened, either by the noise of the wood which continued to fall or by the loud cries of the family, who came together to the spot. At last, being awakened by those who pushed and pulled him, he began to lament and complain that he had been awakened from a sweet and quiet sleep, declaring that he had been sleeping most sweetly in the arms of the Blessed Francis. But when they showed him from how great a height he had fallen to the ground, seeing that he was at the bottom of the tower, at the top of which he had laid down, he was astonished at what had happened to him while he was wholly unconscious of it; and he promised, in the presence of all, to do penance to the honor of God and St. Francis.

In a city called Pofo, in Campagna, a Priest, named Thomas, wished to rebuild a mill which belonged to

the church, and passing heedlessly along the edge of
the canal, where the water was very deep, he suddenly
and unexpectedly fell into it, and got entangled in the
wheel which turned the mill; and thus, being fastened
to the wood, he was turned round and round, the water
falling with great impetuosity upon his face, so that
he had not breath to cry, but he invoked St. Francis
in his heart, and remaining thus for a long time
stretched upon the wheel, his companions despaired
of his life, when they saw the wheel going round with
great violence, and the poor Priest, struggling and pant-
ing, plunged thus miserably in the water. And, behold,
a Friar Minor, clothed in a white tunic, and girded
with a cord, drew him very gently out of the water by
the arm, saying, "I am Francis, whom thou hast
invoked." The Priest, seeing himself thus delivered,
was filled with wonder, and wishing to kiss the feet of
his deliverer, sought anxiously for him on every side,
saying to his companions, "Where is he? whither went
the Saint?" Then these men cast themselves trembling
upon the ground, praising the glorious works of the
great God, and the merits and virtues of His humble
servant Francis.

A certain young man of Borgo-a-Celano went into the
meadows to mow the grass. In those meadows was an
ancient well, covered with grass, which had so concealed
its mouth that it was hidden from all passers-by, the
depth of it being about four paces. The mowers coming
together from different parts, one of them accidentally
fell into the well. While his body was buried therein,
he raised his heart and mind on high to ask the aid of
the Blessed Francis, and as he was falling, cried out
with faith and confidence, "St. Francis, help me!" The
others, who were seeking him hither and thither, and
could nowhere find him, began to lament over him with
cries and tears. Having at last discovered that he had

fallen into the well, they returned weeping to Borgo, to tell what had befallen him, and to ask help. Returning to the place with a great multitude, they let down a rope into the well, and saw the young man sitting upon the water, having suffered no injury therefrom. When he was drawn forth from the well, he said to all the bystanders, "As soon as I fell, I called for aid to the Blessed Francis, who, as I was falling to the bottom, suddenly lifted me up with his hand, nor did he ever leave me until, together with you, he had drawn me out of the well."

In the Church of St. Francis, in the city of Assisi, the Bishop of Ostia, who was afterwards Pope Alexander, was preaching before the Roman Court, when a large and heavy stone, which had been inadvertently left over the high marble pulpit, suddenly fell upon the head of a lady who was listening to the sermon. All who were present, supposing that her head was broken, and that she was already dead, covered her with a mantle which she had about her, that she might be carried forth to burial at the end of the sermon. But she had faithfully commended herself to the Blessed Francis, at the foot of whose altar she lay. And no sooner was the sermon ended, than the lady rose in presence of them all, in such perfect health that not the slightest sign of injury was visible. And what is more marvellous still, having for many years before suffered almost continually from intense pain in the head, she was from that day forward perfectly freed from that infirmity, as she herself afterwards testified.

In the city of Corneto, a bell was to be founded for the Friars Minor; certain devout men came to see it, and among them a boy of eight years old, named Bartholomew, was bringing refreshments to the Friars who were laboring at the work. Suddenly, a violent wind arose which shook the roof, and lifted the door from its hinges; it was very large and heavy, and fell with such violence upon the boy that, as all believed, he was crushed beneath its weight; it so entirely covered him that no part of his body was visible. All who were present ran to the spot, invoking the power of the blessed right hand of St. Francis. But the father, whose limbs had become cold and rigid with grief, being unable to move, offered his son with loud cries and prayers to St. Francis. The heavy weight was at last raised from the body of the child, and, behold, he who was supposed to be dead appeared all smiling, as if he had just awoke from sleep, and bearing no mark of injury. When he had attained his fourteenth year, he joined the Order of Friars Minor, and became a learned and famous preacher.

The men of the city of Lantino had cut a great stone from a mountain, which was to be placed under the altar in the church of St. Francis, then about to be consecrated; about forty men were employed to place the said stone upon a cart, and having several times endeavored to do so with all their strength, the stone fell upon one of them, who was buried beneath it. Not knowing what to do, and being all confounded in mind, the greater number departed in despair; ten alone remained, who lamentably called upon St. Francis, praying him that he would not suffer anyone to perish thus horribly in his service; at last they took courage, and raised the stone with so much ease, that no one doubted the presence of the power of St. Francis, and the man arose alive and sound in all his limbs; and, moreover, having been before short-sighted, he recovered the full and clear use of his eyes, so that all might know how mighty are the merits of St. Francis in the most desperate cases.

A similar thing happened near San Severino, in the Marches of Ancona. A number of men were drawing an immense stone, brought from Constantinople, for the church of St. Francis. The stone suddenly fell upon one of them; and while the rest believed that he was not only dead, but crushed to pieces, by the help of the Blessed Francis, who raised the stone, the man arose safe and well.

Bartholomew, a citizen of Gaeta, had labored much to build a church in honor of St. Francis, when a beam, which had been insecurely fastened, fell and grievously hurt him. Feeling that his head was broken, and that he was nigh unto death, he, being a devout and pious man, besought one of the Friars to bring him the Most Holy Sacrament. The Friar, fearing that there would not be time, because his death was so near at hand, said to him, in the words of St. Augustine: "*Believe, and thou hast eaten.*" On the following night St. Francis appeared to him, in company with eleven Friars, bearing a lamb in his bosom; and standing by the bed, he called him by his name: "Bartholomew," he said, "fear not, for the enemy can do nothing against thee. He has sought to hinder thee in my service, but behold the Lamb for Whom thou didst ask, Whom by reason of thy good desire thou hast received, and by Whose power thou shalt likewise obtain the healing both of thy body and thy soul." And then, laying his hand upon the wounds, he commanded him to return on the morrow to the work he had begun. Then, in the morning, he rose very early, and showing himself to those who had left him for dead, they were filled with wonder and admiration to behold him full of joy and health, and were excited by his example, and by the sight of the miracle, to great love and reverence for the Blessed Father.

A man of Ceperano, named Nicolas, fell one day into the hands of some cruel enemies, who inflicted many terrible wounds upon him, and then left him at the point of death. As soon as he felt himself wounded,

Nicolas began to cry with a loud voice, "St. Francis, help me! St. Francis, aid me!" and these cries were heard by many who were at too great a distance to be able to help him. He was brought to his house, all bathed in his own blood, yet he confidently affirmed that he should not die of those wounds, and that he then felt no pain from them, for that St. Francis had helped him, and had obtained for him from the Lord time to do penance for his sins. And the truth of his words was confirmed by what came to pass. For when the blood was washed away, the man, contrary to all human expectation, was found free from injury.

The son of a nobleman at Geminiano was suffering under a grievous and hopeless malady, which had reduced him to extreme misery. A stream of blood flowed continually from his eyes, such as is wont to issue from the opening of a vein in the arm; and all other indications of approaching death appearing, he lay devoid of power, sense, or motion, so that he was believed by all to be in his agony. The parents and friends, according to custom, gathered together weeping, and discoursed concerning his burial; but his father, having faith in the Lord, hastened to the church of St. Francis, which was near to the place, and placing a cord round his neck, humbly prostrated himself upon the ground, and with many prayers, tears, and sighs besought St. Francis to be his advocate with Christ. No sooner had the father returned home, than his weeping was turned to joy, for he found his son restored to perfect health.

A similar miracle was wrought by the Lord, through the merits of the Saint, on a maiden in a town called Thamarit, not far from Ancona, in Catalonia, who, being near to death from the extremity of her sickness, was restored to perfect health when her parents devoutly invoked the Blessed Francis.

A certain clerk at Vico-Albo, named Matthew, having

drunk of some poisonous drink, lost the use of his speech, and seemed at the last extremity. A priest came to hear his confession, but he could not utter a single word. But having humbly raised his heart to Christ, he besought Him, by the merits of the Blessed Francis, to deliver him from the jaws of death. Immediately, being strengthened by the Lord, he pronounced the name of St. Francis with faithful devotion, and having rejected the poison in the presence of many witnesses, he returned thanks to his deliverer.

Of many who were Delivered from Shipwreck.

ERTAIN mariners were in great danger by sea, about ten miles from the port of Baruti, and, the tempest waxing fiercer and fiercer, they began to fear for their lives, and cast anchor in the sea. But the sea rose higher still by the fury of the wind and the storm, so that the ropes were broken, and they were left without an anchor, wandering in an uncertain and unequal course over the waves. At last, by the Divine Will, the sea was calmed, and they endeavored with all their power to recover the anchor, the ropes of which they saw floating on the sea. Unable to do this by their own strength, they invoked the aid of many Saints, and, worn out with toil and labor, they were unable, in the course of a whole day, to recover a single anchor. Now there was one of the sailors, named Perfetto (Perfect), but in his manner of life very imperfect, who said in derision to his companions: "See, you have been calling all the Saints to aid, and, as you see, not one of them helps us. Let us ask this Francis, who is a new Saint; perhaps he will dive into the water and recover our lost anchors." They all agreed to the advice of Perfetto, not in jest, but truly and faithfully, and, reproving his impious words, they turned of their own accord to the Saint, and in a moment, without any human help, they saw the anchors floating upon the water, as if the nature of iron had been changed into the lightness of wood.

A certain pilgrim, reduced to great weakness of body by the effects of a severe fever, was brought in a ship from the parts beyond the sea. He had a special affection and devotion to St. Francis, whom he had chosen as his advocate with the Heavenly King. Not being yet perfectly free from his sickness, he was tormented by a burning thirst, and there being no water in the ship, he began to cry aloud: "Go with all confidence and bring me a cup, for St. Francis has filled my little barrel." Marvellous to say they found the barrel filled with water, which had before been perfectly empty. Another day, a tempest arose, and filled the ship with waves, so that, by reason of the violence of the storm, all on board began to fear shipwreck, when the sick man arose suddenly and cried throughout the ship; "Arise, all of you, and go and meet the Blessed Francis; behold, he is coming to salute us!" And crying thus with a loud voice and many tears, he fell on his face and adored him. And immediately, at the vision of the Saint, the sick man recovered his health, and the sea was calmed.

Brother James, of Rieti, was passing a streamlet in a little boat; when it approached the land, and his companions had disembarked, he was about to follow them, but the little bark being accidentally overturned, the brother fell into the water. The brethren on the shore besought the Blessed Francis, with many tears, to deliver his son. And the Friar at the bottom of the river, being unable to cry with his mouth, called upon his merciful Father as best he could in his heart. And, behold, by the present aid of the Blessed Father, he walked as on dry land, in the bottom of the stream, and taking hold of the sunken boat, he brought it with him to the shore. Wonderful to say, his garments were not wet, not was there a drop of water on his tunic.

Another Friar, named Bonaventure, was rowing with two other brothers on a certain lake, when the boat, being broken by the force of the current, sank with himself and his companions to the bottom. When, from this lake of misery, they called with confidence on their merciful Father Francis, the boat, full of water, rose to the surface, and, by the guidance of the Saint, reached the harbor in safety.

Thus also another Friar of Escolo, who had fallen into a river, was delivered by the merits of St. Francis.

Several men and women in a like peril on the Lake of Rieti, by the invocation of the name of St. Francis, escaped the danger of shipwreck.

Some mariners of Ancona, being attacked by a dangerous tempest, were in danger of being swallowed up by the waves. When, despairing of life, they devoutly invoked the aid of St. Francis, a great light appeared over the sea, and with that light there was granted te them, by the divine mercy, a great calm, as if the holy man by his marvellous power could command the winds and the sea. Now it is not possible, I think, to relate, if I would, all the wonders by which our Blessed Father has been glorified, and is now glorified, in the deep. Nor is it any marvel that to him, who already reigns in Heaven, is given power to command the waters, seeing that all living creatures served him while he was yet in this mortal life.

Of many who were Delivered from Chains and Dungeons.

T happened in Romagna that a certain Greek, a servant to a great person in that country, was falsely accused of theft, and immediately imprisoned by the lord of the country in a dark dungeon and strongly bound. But the lady of the house in which he served, moved with compassion for the poor servant, whom she fully believed to be innocent of any crime, earnestly and constantly besought her lord and husband to set him free. Then, being unable to move the hard obstinacy of her husband, the lady had recourse to St. Francis, and devoutly recommending the innocent man to the mercy of the Saint, she made a vow for his deliverance. Then the protector of the miserable man, with great compassion, visited the innocent prisoner in his dungeon. He loosed his bands, opened the prison door, and taking him by the hand, he led him forth, saying, "I am he to whom thy mistress devoutly commended thee." Then the poor man, being seized with great fear, and seeking for some pathway down the precipice upon which he stood, suddenly found himself, by the power of his deliverer, on the plain below. Then he returned to his mistress, and relating the miracle in order to her, inflamed the heart of the devout lady to a still more fervent love of Christ, and greater reverence for His servant Francis.

There was a poor man at Massa, who owed a certain sum of money to a knight of San Pietra, and being unable in his poverty to pay it when the said knight suddenly demanded it of him, he humbly besought him to have mercy on him, and, for the love of St. Francis, to grant him a little delay. But the proud knight despised the prayers of the poor man, and set at nought the love of the Saint, as if it were a vain thing. And thus in his obstinacy he answered him, "I will confine thee in so close a prison, and in so remote a place, that neither Francis nor anyone else shall be able to help thee;" and he was as good as his word, for he found a dark dungeon, into which he cast the poor man strongly bound. Soon afterwards St. Francis came, and throwing open the dungeon, and breaking his fetters, he brought the poor man safe home to his own house. Thus the might of St. Francis overcame the haughty knight, and delivered the prisoner from his captivity, and the pride of the obstinate soldier was changed by the marvellous miracle into meekness.

Albert of Arezzo, having been detained in cruel bonds for some debts which were unjustly demanded of him, devoutly commended his innocence to St. Francis, whom he held in veneration above all the saints, having a special affection also to the Order of Friars Minor. His creditor said to him, with words of blasphemy, that neither Francis nor God should deliver him out of his hands. On the vigil of St. Francis, the prisoner had eaten nothing, having, for the love of the Saint, given his portion of food to a poor man; and as he was watching on the following night, St. Francis appeared to him. On his entrance, the chains immediately fell from his hands and the fetters from his feet. The doors opened of their own accord, and the poor man, being set free, returned to his home. From that day he kept the vow which he had now made, fasting always on the vigil of St. Francis; and the wax-taper, which he was accustomed to offer him every year, he thenceforward, in token of the increase of his devotion, increased by the weight of an ounce.

When Pope Gregory IX was sitting in the chair of St. Peter, a certain man named Peter, of the city of Alesia, on an accusation of heresy, was carried to Rome, and, by command of the same Pontiff, was given in custody to the Bishop of Tivoli. He, having been charged to keep him in safety, under penalty of the loss of his bishopric, bound him with heavy chains, and imprisoned him in a dark dungeon, from which there was no possible means of escape, giving him food and drink by measure and weight. This man began to call with many prayers and tears upon St. Francis, the vigil of whose Feast was close at hand, beseeching him to have mercy upon him. And because, by the purity of faith, all error of heretical pravity had been driven from his heart when he turned to Francis, the faithful servant of Christ, he was made worthy by his merits to be heard by the Lord. For, about twilight on the vigil of his Feast, St. Francis mercifully appeared to him in his prison, and, calling him by his name, commanded him immediately to arise. He, being full of fear, asked who it was that spoke to him, and was told that it was the Blessed Francis. Then, by the power of the presence of the holy man, he beheld the fetters fall broken from his feet, and the doors of the prison were unlocked without anyone to open them, so that he could go forth unbound and free; nevertheless, being full of wonder, he durst not go forth, but calling at the doors, affrighted all the jailers. Then they made known to the bishop that he had been set free from all bonds, and when the devout prelate understood the matter in order, he came to the prison, and seeing the power of God thus manifest, he acknowledged it, and adored the Lord. Some of the chains were brought to the Pope and the cardinals, who, beholding what had been done, blessed God in wonder and admiration.

Guido-lotto, of San Geminiano, was falsely accused of having poisoned a certain man, and of intending by the same means to destroy his son and all his family. Being apprehended by the magistrate of the place, he was loaded with heavy chains and shut up in a tower. But knowing his own innocence, and having confidence in the Lord, he committed the defense of his cause to St. Francis. The magistrate casting in his mind by what manner of torments he might draw from him the confession of his crime, and by what punishment, when he should have confessed it, he would put him to death, the prisoner, on the night before he was to be led forth to torture, was visited by the presence of St. Francis, and surrounded by a great glory even until the morning, so that, being filled with great joy and confidence, he felt sure of his deliverance. In the morning they who were to torture him came and brought him forth from the prison, and put him to the torture, loading him with many heavy chains to increase his pains. He was many times raised from the earth and cast down again, that, by torture succeeding torture, he might be the sooner brought to confess his crime. But the spirit of innocence shone brightly in his face, nor did he seem to experience any pain. Then a great fire was lighted under him, over which he was hung by the feet, with his head downwards, yet not a hair of his head was singed. Lastly, he was covered with boiling oil, which was poured over his body, and he overcame all these torments by the power of that patron to whom he had committed his defense, and so he was set free, and departed safe and sound.

Of many Women who were Delivered from the Danger of Childbirth.

CERTAIN Countess in Sclavonia, illustrious for her birth, and an imitator of the virtues of St. Francis, was full of devotion towards him, and of great piety and charity towards his whole Order. Having come once upon a time to the hour of her delivery, she endured such terrible and grievous pains, that it seemed as if the birth of the child must be the death of the mother. It seemed that the child could not obtain its life but by the sacrifice of the life of the mother, and that the hour of her delivery must be the hour of her death. Being in such peril, a thought came into her mind of the fame, the virtue, and the glory of

St. Francis, which so excited her faith and inflamed her devotion, that she turned to him, the effectual and faithful friend, the consolation of the devout, and the refuge of the afflicted. "St. Francis," she said, "all my bones supplicate thy mercy, and with my heart I vow to thee what with my lips I cannot express." Oh! marvellous and speedy effect of piety! The end of her speech was the end also of her sorrow, and the beginning of her labor was the end thereof; for her pains immediately ceased, and she brought forth her child in safety. Nor was she forgetful of her vow, or unfaithful to her promise. For she built a fair church in honor of the Saint, and gave it to the Friars of his Order.

There was a woman in the neighborhood of Rome, named Beatrice, who had borne for four days a dead child within her womb, and was suffering the agonies of death. That which was already dead was bringing the mother to death. The physicians tried their art in vain, but all human remedy seemed fruitless, so that the curse of Eve had fallen with unwonted severity upon the head of this unhappy woman, who, having become the sepulchre of her child, was fast hastening to her own. At last she commended herself with great devotion to the Friars Minor, beseeching them with full faith to send her some relic of St. Francis. By the Will of God they found a piece of cord, with which the Saint had girded himself, which was no sooner laid upon the woman than she was delivered of the dead child which had brought her nigh to death, and restored to her former health.

Guiliana, the wife of a nobleman of Como, was full of sorrow at the death of her children, and wept continually over her unhappy case, because all the children whom with great sorrow she had brought forth, in a short space of time, with no less sorrow, she saw carried forth to their grave. Being now within five months of her delivery, because of the misfortune which had befallen her other children she was more solicitous concerning the death of her expected infant than concerning its birth; therefore she faithfully besought the Blessed Father St. Francis for the life of her unborn child. And behold, as she was asleep one night, a woman appeared to her bearing a beautiful child in her arms, which with a joyful countenance she presented to her. And when she refused to receive it, fearing lest she should forthwith lose it again, the woman said to her: "Take it, and fear not, for St. Francis, who has had pity on thy sorrow, hath sent it to thee; the child shall live and gladden thee by its health." Then the lady awoke, and understood by this vision from Heaven that the aid of St. Francis would be present with her, and being filled with great joy, she began to pray more intensely and fervently for the child which had been promised her. When the time came that she should bring forth, the lady gave birth to a boy, who, by his infantine strength and beauty, seemed to have received the food of life by the merits of St. Francis; and thus were his parents excited to a still greater devotion towards Christ and His Saint.

A similar grace was bestowed by the holy Father in the city of Tivoli. A woman there, who had already many daughters, having a great desire for a son, began to offer prayers and vows to St. Francis. By his merits, the woman who had prayed for one son only, gave birth to two.

A woman at Viterbo, who was near her delivery, seemed nearer still to her death, being tormented with every kind of sorrow and pain to which women are subject at such times. When nature seemed sinking under them, and every art of medicine had been tried in vain, the woman called upon the name of St. Francis, and was forthwith safely delivered. Having obtained her desire, she forgot the benefit received, and instead of paying due honor to the Saint, she began to work on his Festival, when, behold! her right arm, which she had stretched forth to labor, remained withered and stiff. When she tried to draw it towards her with the other, that also, by a similar punishment, was dried up. The woman, being seized with fear from on high, renewed her vow, and by the merits of the merciful and humble Saint, to whom she again commended herself, she recovered the use of her limbs, which by her contempt and ingratitude she had lost.

Another woman, from the neighborhood of Arezzo, had been seven days in the perils of childbirth; she had already turned black, and being given over by all, she devoted herself to St. Francis, and began to invoke his aid in death. She had no sooner done so than she fell asleep, and in a dream beheld St. Francis, who spoke to her most sweetly, asking her whether she knew him, and whether she could say the *Salve Regina* in honor of the glorious Virgin. When she replied that she knew it, "Begin," said the Saint, "the sacred Antiphon, and before thou hast finished it thou shalt bring forth in safety." At these words the woman awoke, and began with great fear to say the *Salve Regina,* and when she came to those words, "*Illos tuos misericordes oculos,*" and made mention of the Fruit of that virginal womb, she was immediately delivered from all her pains, and brought forth a beautiful infant, giving thanks to the Queen of Mercy, who, by the merits of the Blessed Francis, had vouchsafed to have compassion on her.

Of many Blind who were Restored to Sight.

N the Convent of the Friars Minor, at Naples, there was a certain Friar named Robert, who had been many years blind, and there had lately grown over his eyes a superfluity of flesh, which hindered the motion and use of the eyelids. Now, many foreign Friars came to this place, being brought together from divers parts by the will of the Blessed Father St. Francis, that the miracle might thus take place in the presence of many; and thus was the brother healed. One night the said Brother Robert was lying in his bed sick unto death, and his soul had been already commended to God, when, behold! he saw the Blessed Father before him, with three Friars full of sanctity, and these were St. Anthony, Br. Augustine, and Br. James, of Assisi, who, as they had so perfectly followed him during life, now bore him company after death. Then St. Francis, taking a knife, began to cut away that superfluous flesh, and restored to him his lost sight, raising him also from death to life. Then he said to him: "My son, Friar Robert, the grace which I have bestowed upon thee is a token to these brethren who are going into distant countries, that I will always go before them and direct their steps—therefore, let them depart in gladness, and perform with a willing mind the obedience imposed upon them."

At Thebes, in Romagna, a blind woman, having fasted on bread and water on the vigil of St. Francis, was led by her husband on the morning of the Feast to the church of the Friars Minor. And when the Mass was celebrated, at the elevation of the Body of Christ, she saw It clearly, and most devoutly adored It, crying with a loud voice: "Thanks be to God and His Saint, for I see the Body of Christ." All those who were

present turned to see whence that joyful voice pro-
ceeded, and when the Mass was ended, the woman
returned to her house, rejoicing in spirit and with the
sight of her eyes. And she rejoiced not only because
she had received her bodily sight, but because, by the
merits of St. Francis and by the aid of holy faith, she
had beheld that stupendous Sacrament which is the
light of the living soul.

At a place called Poffo, in Campagna, there was a
boy of fourteen, who, by a sudden infirmity, entirely
lost the use of his left eye, and the intensity of the
pain so removed the eye out of its place that, the nerves
being relaxed by a finger's length, it hung for a whole
week down the cheek, being almost entirely dried up.
There remained no other remedy but to cut it off, and
the physicians being hopeless of a cure, he turned with
all his mind to ask the assistance of St. Francis. Nor
did that prompt helper of the miserable delay to grant
the prayer of his suppliant, for, by his marvellous power,
he restored the withered eye to its place and to its former strength, illuminating it with the longed-for light
of day.

In the same province, at a place called Magno, a
heavy piece of wood fell from a great height, and struck
the head of a certain Priest, blinding him in the left
eye. As he lay on the ground, he began to invoke St.
Francis, saying: "Help me, most holy Father, so that I
may be able to go to thy Festival, as I have promised
thy Friars;" for it was the vigil of the Saint, and when
he had said this, he immediately arose safe and sound,
and began to praise God, rejoicing with all around, who
had been lamenting his misfortune, and were now filled
with joy and wonder. He went to the Feast and related
to all the power and mercy which he had experienced.

Another man of Mount Gorgano, who was laboring
in his vineyard, injured his eye as he was cutting a

piece of wood, dividing it so that the half of it hung out of the socket. Despairing of all human aid, he made a vow to St. Francis always to fast before his Feast if he would help him now. The Saint immediately restored the eye to its proper place, and restored also its lost sight, so that not a vestige of the injury remained.

The son of a nobleman, who was born blind, received his sight by the merits of St. Francis, and from this cause received the name of Illuminato. When he grew up, in thanksgiving for the benefit received, he took the habit of St. Francis, and made such progress in the life of grace and holiness that he showed himself to be truly a child of light, and by the merits of the holy Father he ended his life by a still holier death.

At Zacanto, near Anagna, there was a soldier, named Gerard, who had altogether lost his sight. It happened once that two Friars Minor, from distant parts, came to lodge with him; and having been devoutly received and kindly treated, out of reverence for St. Francis, they thanked God and their host, and went their way to a convent of Friars not far from that place. One night St. Francis appeared to one of these Friars in a dream, saying: "Arise, and go quickly with thy companion to the house of our host, who received Christ and me in your persons, for I wish to requite him for his good offices He became blind because of his sins, which he cared not to purge by confession." When the Father had said this he disappeared, and the Friar immediately arose with his companion to fulfill the commandment laid upon him. And when they came to the house of the hospitable man, they related to him in order the vision which one of them had seen, which, when he had heard, he marvelled greatly; and acknowledging that to be true which they said, and being contrite even to tears, he willingly made his confession. Being thus corrected and renewed, and restored to sight in the interior man, he forthwith recovered his exterior sight; and the fame of that miracle being spread abroad through all the country round, excited many not only to reverence for the Saint, but also to humble confession of their sins, and to loving hospitality to the poor.

Of many who were Delivered from Divers Infirmities.

T a place called Pieve, there was a poor beggarboy who had been deaf and dumb from his birth, and whose tongue was so short that those who examined his mouth thought that it must have been even cut off. A certain man, named Mark, received him into his house for the love of God: and he, finding himself so well off there, continued to abide with him. One day, when the man was supping with his wife (the child being with them), he said to his wife: "I should assuredly hold it to be a great miracle if the Blessed Francis would restore this child's hearing and speech;" adding, "I vow to God that if St. Francis will do this, for the love of him, I will support this child as long as he lives." Marvellous to say, the tongue immediately began to grow and the child spoke, saying: "Glory be to God, and to St. Francis."

Brother James, of Iseo, when he was a child in his father's house, sustained a grievous bodily injury. But by the inspiration of the Holy Ghost, although so feeble in health, he entered very young into the Order of St. Francis, disclosing to none the infirmity under which he labored. Now it happened that when the body of St. Francis was transported to the place where the precious treasure of his sacred bones was to be preserved, the said Friar was present at the festival of the translation, desiring to do due honor to his glorious Father. He approached the sepulchre in which the sacred body lay, and embraced it in the fervor of his devotion, when he immediately felt himself restored to health, and from that moment was set free from his infirmity.

By the mercy of God and the merits of St. Francis, the same marvellous cure was vouchsafed to many others, among whom were Br. Bartolo of Gubbio, Br. Angelo of Toli, a Priest of Stichiano, named Nicholas, John of Fora, a certain man from Pisa, another from Ciperna, Peter of Sicily, and another from Spello, in the neighborhood of Assisi.

There was a woman in the Maremma who had been for five years out of her mind, being also both blind and deaf; she would often tear her clothes with her teeth and throw herself into the water or the fire, and became at last subject to dreadful attacks of epilepsy. Now it happened by the disposal of the divine mercy, that one night a divine light shone around her, and in a dream she saw St. Francis seated upon a lofty throne, before whom she prostrated herself, imploring him to restore her to health. But he seeming not yet to hear her prayers, the woman made a vow, for the love of God and of His Saints, to give alms to whomsoever should ask of her as long as she should have anything to give. The Saint at once accepted the offer, which was the same he himself had once made to the Lord, and making the sign of the Cross over her, he restored her to perfect health.

It is also known for a truth that St. Francis mercifully delivered from the same infirmity a maiden of Norsia, and the son of a certain nobleman, and many others.

Peter of Foligno was on his way to visit the church of St. Michael, but, as he was making the pilgrimage with little reverence, it happened that, as he was drinking at a certain fountain, he was suddenly possessed by the devil, by whom for three years he was miserably tormented, using horrible language, and being terrible to look upon. Having at times lucid intervals, he made use of one of them to go to the sepulchre of the merciful Father to ask his help, for he had heard that it was efficacious against the powers of the air; and no sooner had he touched the sepulchre with his hand than he was delivered from the power of the devil who tormented him.

In like manner the mercy of St. Francis was shown to a woman of Narni, who was likewise possessed, and to many others, whose sufferings and cures it were too long to relate.

There was a man called Buono, of the city of Fano, paralytic and a leper, who was carried by his parents to the church of St. Francis, where he was perfectly healed of both diseases.

Another young man called Atto, of San Severino, who had been struck with leprosy, made a vow to the Saint, and having been carried to his sepulchre, was by his merits perfectly healed. The Saint had a special power in the healing of this disease, because, in his love of piety and humility, he had ever willingly and humbly served the lepers.

A certain noble lady named Rogarda, in the diocese of Soria, had been subject for twenty-three years to an issue of blood, and having suffered much from many physicians, seemed, from the extremity of her pains, to be at the point of death; and if the blood stopped flowing for a time, her body swelled in a most frightful manner. Now, it happened one day that she heard a boy singing in the Latin tongue the miracles which God had wrought by the Blessed Father St. Francis, and being moved with sorrow she burst into tears, and began to say with great faith: "Oh, Blessed Father St. Francis, who art glorified by so many miracles, if thou wilt vouchsafe to deliver me from this disease, it will bring thee a great increase of glory, for thou hast never wrought such a miracle as this." What more shall I say? She had no sooner spoken these words than, by the merits of the Blessed Francis, she felt that she was healed. Her son also, whose name was Mark, had an arm contracted, and when he had made a vow to St. Francis, it was perfectly restored.

A woman of Sicily, who had labored for seven years under an issue of blood, was made whole by the Standard-bearer of Christ.

In the city of Rome there was a woman named Praseda, well known for her piety and holiness of life. From her earliest youth she had shut herself up for the love of Christ, her Spouse, for the space of forty years, in a narrow cell near to the church of St. Francis, whence she desired to obtain from him a signal grace. For having got upon the window-sill of her cell for some necessary purpose, she was taken with a strange giddiness, and fell, breaking her leg in two places, and dislocating her shoulder. Then our most benign Father appeared to her, clothed in dazzling raiment of light, and began thus sweetly to speak to her: "Arise," he said, "blessed daughter, arise and fear not." And taking her by the hand he raised her up, and immediately disappeared. Then she, seeking hither and thither, throughout her cell, thought she had seen a vision, until, at her cries, a light was brought to her, and she felt that she was perfectly cured by Francis, the servant of God, and related in order all that had happened to her.

Of some who observed not the Saint's Festival,
and paid him not due Honor.

N a place called Simo, in the neighborhood of Pavia, there was a Priest called Reginald, who was very devout to St. Francis, and exhorted his parishioners to keep his Feast with great solemnity. But one of the people, being ignorant of the virtues of the Saint, set at nought the Priest's command. He went out into the field to cut wood, and as he prepared to work he heard a voice saying to him three times: "It is a Feast: it is not lawful to work." But neither the command of the Priest nor the words of the divine oracle could restrain his rashness; therefore, the divine power and the glory of the Saint were shown forth by a miraculous punishment. For as he held with one hand the wood which he was about to cut, and in the other the hatchet which was to cut it, by the divine power both hands were so firmly attached to what they held that he could neither open his hands nor stretch out his fingers. Being then in great astonishment, and knowing not what to do, he went thus to the church, whither many accompanied him to see the marvellous prodigy. Prostrating himself, therefore, with all humility before the altar, according to the direction of the Priest, who was present (for many Priests had come thither to celebrate the Feast), he humbly made a threefold vow to St. Francis, corresponding to the three voices which he had heard: 1) That he would always devoutly celebrate his Festival. 2) That on the day of his Festival he would always visit that church in which he now was. 3) That he would make a pilgrimage in person to the body of the Saint. Wonderful to relate, no sooner had he made one vow, than he was able to move one of his fingers; at the second, another; and at the third, a third; and then the whole hand, and afterwards the other hand; while the great multitude of people who were gathered together were devoutly imploring mercy from the Saint. The man, being thus restored to his former health, of his own accord laid the tools of which he had made use before the altar of the Saint, where they may be seen to this day; and all the people praised God and extolled the great power of the Saint, who was so mighty to smite and to heal. And many miracles wrought there and in many neighboring places testify to the glory of the Saint in Heaven, and that his Feast should be devoutly celebrated by all men upon earth.

In the city of Como, on the Feast of St. Francis, a woman, setting about to spin, stretched her hands out to the distaff, and took the spindle in her fingers, when her hands became quite stiff, and she was seized with a violent pain in her fingers; when, recognizing the power of the Saint in her punishment, she went with great compunction of heart to the Friars. And while the devout sons were praying for her recovery, by the clemency of the holy Father she was made perfectly whole. Nor did any pain or scar remain on her hands, except a slight mark, as of a burn, in memory of the miracle.

In like manner another woman in the Campagna, a second in a place called Oleto, and another at Pilci, who had despised the Saint's Festival, were miraculously punished for their error, and on their repentance, by the merits of St. Francis, were miraculously healed.

A certain soldier at Borgo profanely spoke evil of the works and miracles of St. Francis, abused the pilgrims who came to visit his sepulchre, and publicly reproached the friars with foolish words. Now, it happened one day that, when he was thus assailing the honor of the Saint, he added to his other sins this detestable blasphemy: "If it be true," he said, "that this Francis is a Saint, let me now die, and if he be not a Saint I shall remain uninjured." The anger of God was not slow to inflict a due punishment upon a prayer thus made in sin, for not long afterwards, as this blasphemer was insulting one of his nephews, the young man drew his sword and pierced him to the heart and thus on that same day died this miserable slave of hell and son of darkness, that others might learn that the marvellous works of St. Francis are not to be blasphemously assailed, but devoutly honored.

A certain judge, named Alexander, having with a venomous tongue sought to lessen the devotion to St. Francis, was, by the judgment of God, deprived of the use of his tongue, and remained speechless for six years together. He, being tormented in the member which had sinned, was moved to great penance, and sorrowed greatly that he had spoken against the miracles of the Saint. Therefore the anger of the merciful Saint was appeased, and being reconciled to the penitent judge, who humbly asked his aid, he restored to him his speech; and thenceforward the tongue which had been full of curses was consecrated to the honor of the Saint, from whom he had received this discipline, and at the same time the grace of devotion.

Of many Miracles of Various Kinds.

T Galialo was a woman named Mary, who was most devout to our Lord and to St. Francis. It happened that on one summer's day she left her house in search of necessary food, and the heat being very great, she began to faint with thirst; being unable to find anything to drink, for she was alone on a barren mountain, she fell upon the ground half dead, and began fervently and piously to call upon her advocate,

St. Francis. The devout woman persevered long in her humble prayer, and being overcome with weariness, heat, and thirst, she fell asleep, when, behold St. Francis appeared to her, and, calling her by her name, said to her: "Arise, and drink this water, which God gives to thee and to many others." At these words the woman arose from sleep, no little comforted, and taking a stone which lay near, she broke it, and hollowed out the earth therewith; and then boring with a stick, she came to living water, which at first appearing but a little stream, by the divine power grew to an abundant fountain. The woman drank thereof, and when she had quenched her thirst, she washed her eyes therewith, which, having been long dimmed by a weakness of sight, now received new light and strength. Then the woman ran to her house and made known the stupendous miracle, to the glory of St. Francis. Many came from all parts for the fame of this miracle, and learned by experience the marvellous virtue of this water; for everyone who touched it, if he had first confessed his sins, was delivered thereby from whatsoever disease he had. And even to this day this fountain may be seen; and an oratory has been built in that place in honor of St. Francis.

At St. Jacondo, in Spain, a cherry-tree, belonging to a worthy man, had withered; and the Saint, against all hope, restored it to its pristine life, causing it to bring forth leaves, flowers, and fruit.

All the vineyards in the neighborhood of Vilesi were delivered by his marvellous help from the worms and vermin which preyed upon them.

A Priest, near Valencia, whose granaries were every year emptied by the moths and other vermin, fervently implored the help of the Saint, who entirely freed him from this plague.

The lands of a nobleman in Apulia having been commended to his care, he preserved them entirely from the grubs which infested all the neighboring fields.

There was a certain man named Martin, who, having led his cattle to pasture, at some distance from his house, the leg of one of them was so grievously broken that it seemed past remedy. Desiring to bind up the leg and set it, and having no bandage for the purpose, he went back to his house to find one, committing his ox, in the meantime, to the care and custody of St. Francis, beseeching him with great confidence that he would not suffer it to be devoured by the wolves during his absence. The next morning he returned early to his ox, bringing the butcher with him, and found it quietly grazing, so perfectly restored to health that he could not discern the broken leg from the others. And so he returned thanks to the Good Shepherd who had so lovingly cared for and cured his beast.

This humble Saint is wont to succor all those who call upon him in any necessity, however trifling it may be. For he restored to a man of Amiterno a horse which had been stolen from him; and to a woman of Interduco, who had let fall a basin upon the ground, and broken it into many pieces, he restored it whole. He also made whole a ploughshare belonging to a man named Mark, at Olmo, which had been broken in pieces.

In the diocese of Subina there was an old woman, eighty years of age, whose daughter died, leaving a child at the breast. This poor old woman was full of trouble, and knew not whither to turn, for she had no milk, nor could she find any woman to give suck to the child. The infant was wasting away, when one night, being abandoned by all human aid, she turned, full of tears, to St. Francis, imploring his aid, when the lover of innocence suddenly stood before her, and said to her: "Oh, woman, I am Francis, whom, with so many tears, thou hast invoked. Place the child's mouth at thy breast, for the Lord will give thee milk in abundance." The old woman did according to the command of the Saint, and forthwith the breasts of a woman of eighty were filled with great abundance of milk. The marvellous gift of the Saint was soon made known abroad, and many, both men and women, came together to the sight, nor could the tongue deny that to which the eye bore witness, so that all were moved to praise God with marvellous and loving devotion for the power of His Saint.

In Spoleto a man and his wife had one only son, over whom they mourned continually as the misfortune of their house. For his arms were attached to his neck, his knees joined to his breast, and his feet to his thighs, so that he seemed rather like a brute monster than a human being. The mother, in the greatness of her affliction, turned with continual weeping to Christ, and invoked the aid of St. Francis, that he would be pleased to help her in her misery and shame. One night when she had fallen into a deep sleep for very sorrow, St. Francis appeared to her, and, comforting her with sweet words, he bade her carry her child to a place hard by, which was dedicated to his name, and there to bathe him in the water of the well, so should he recover perfect health in the Name of the Lord. But she neglecting to fulfill the command of the Saint, he appeared to her a second time, and repeated the same. Then he appeared to her again the third time, and led the woman with her child to the gate of the aforesaid place, guiding them himself; and certain noble matrons, who were going thither from devotion, hearing from this woman of the vision she had seen, went with her to the friars and presented the child to them, and when they came to the well the noblest of the company bathed it therein with their own hands, when the limbs immediately returned to their place, the child was made whole, and the greatness of the miracle filled all men with amazement.

At Chora in the diocese of Ostia, there was a man whose leg was so diseased that he could neither walk nor move. Being in great anguish, and despairing of all human aid, he began one night to lament himself to St. Francis, as if he had been present, crying: "St. Francis, help me! Remember the devout service I have ever rendered thee, for I have made thee ride upon mine ass, I have kissed thy holy hands and feet, and was always most devout and loving to thee, and now by the grievous pain of this leg I am nigh unto death." Moved by his complaints, St. Francis appeared to him, in company with one of his friars, and being mindful of the benefits received from the poor man, and grateful for his devotion, he told him that he had come at his desire, and had brought a remedy to heal him. Then he touched the place of the disease with a little rod, shaped like the letter *Tau*, and the ulcer broke, and he was restored to perfect health. What is more marvellous still, he left upon the healed wound the sacred sign of *Tau* impressed as a memorial of this great miracle. For with this sign St. Francis was wont to sign his letters, which in his charity he wrote to anyone.

And now, behold, as the mind is distracted by the variety of the divers miracles related in this history of the glorious St. Francis, it seems that not without a divine purpose, nor without the consent and will of the glorious Standard-bearer, we come to speak of that holy sign *Tau*. For we may consider that as to him, when he followed Christ militant on earth, it was by the cross that he merited salvation, so now that he triumphs, with Christ is the Cross, the faithful witness of his honor. For this great and marvellous mystery of the Cross, in whose sublime depths are hidden infinite graces and all the treasures of the wisdom and knowledge of God, this mystery which is hidden from the wise and prudent of this world, was to this simple man of Christ so plainly revealed that all his life long he ever followed the footsteps of that Cross, nor did he ever enjoy any sweetness but in the Cross, nor preach any glory but of the Cross: so that from the very beginning of his conversion he could say with the Apostle: "God forbid that I should glory, save in the Cross of our Lord Jesus Christ;" and no less truly could he add in his after-life: "Those who shall follow this rule shall have peace and mercy:" and lastly, in the end, he could say most truly: "I bear in my body the Stigmata of the Lord Jesus." And let it be our daily desire to hear from him: "The grace of our Lord Jesus Christ be with your spirit, brethren. Amen."

Triumph and glory, therefore, now securely, in the glory of the Cross, O glorious Standard-bearer of Christ; for, beginning from the Cross, thou didst go onward according to the rule of the Cross; and being made perfect by the Cross, the faithful have learnt what is thy glory in Heaven by the testimony of the Cross.

Securely let them follow thee who have come out of Egypt, who have passed through the sea divided by the rod of Christ's Cross, and who, going forward through the desert, are carried by the marvellous power of that same holy Cross through the Jordan of our mortality to the Promised Land of the Living. Whither may Jesus Christ, the true Leader and Saviour of His people, bring us all by the merits of His servant Francis! To the praise and glory of Him Who liveth and reigneth, Three Persons in One God, forever and ever. Amen.

If you have enjoyed this book, consider making your next selection from among the following . . .

Prices subject to change.

Prices subject to change.

Prices subject to change.

Prices subject to change.

At your Bookdealer or direct from the Publisher.

Toll-Free 1-800-437-5876   **Fax 815-226-7770**

Tel. 815-226-7777   **www.tanbooks.com**

Prices subject to change.